THE MOST INSPIRING THINGS EVER SAID

THE MOST
Inspiring
THINGS EVER SAID

Edited and with an introduction by
STEVEN D. PRICE

Guilford, Connecticut

An imprint of Globe Pequot

Distributed by NATIONAL BOOK NETWORK
800-462-6420

British Library Cataloguing-in-Publication Information available

Library of Congress Cataloging-in-Publication Data available

ISBN 978-1-4930-2628-9 (paperback)
ISBN 978-1-4930-2623-4 (e-book)

♾™ The paper used in this publication meets the minimum requirements of American National Standard for Information Sciences—Permanence of Paper for Printed Library Materials, ANSI/NISO Z39.48-1992.

ALSO BY THE AUTHOR

* * * * * * * * * * *

Teaching Riding at Summer Camp

Panorama of American Horses

Civil Rights, Volumes 1 and 2

Get a Horse: Basics of Backyard Horsekeeping

Take Me Home: The Rise of Country-and-Western Music

The Second-Time Single Man's Survival Handbook, with William J. Gordon

Old as the Hills: The Story of Bluegrass Music

Horseback Vacation Guide

Schooling to Show: Basics of Hunter-Jumper Training, with Anthony D'Ambrosio, Jr.

The Whole Horse Catalog

The Complete Book of Horse & Saddle Equipment, with Elwyn Hartley Edwards

Riding's a Joy, with Joy Slater

All the King's Horses: The Story of the Budweiser Clydesdales

The Beautiful Baby-Naming Book

Riding for a Fall

The Polo Primer, with Charles Kauffman

The Ultimate Fishing Guide

Caught Me a Big 'un, with Jimmy Houston

The American Quarter Horse

Two Bits' Book of the American Quarter Horse

The Quotable Horse Lover

Essential Riding

The Illustrated Horseman's Dictionary

The Greatest Horse Stories Ever Told

Classic Horse Stories

1001 Smartest Things Ever Said

1001 Dumbest Things Ever Said

1001 Greatest Insults, Put-Downs, and Comebacks

The Best Advice Ever Given

1001 Funniest Things Ever Said

1001 Best Things Ever Said About Horses

1001 Greatest Things Ever Said About California

The Quotable Billionaire

What To Do When a Loved One Dies (republished as *More Than Sympathy*)

The World's Funniest Lawyer Jokes

Endangered Phrases

Excuses for All Occasions

The Little Black Book of Writers' Wisdom

Gut-Busters and Belly Laughs

How to Survive Retirement

TABLE OF CONTENTS

. . . .

INTRODUCTION

. . . .

We have all been inspired at some point in our lives. As a child you may have seen something that caught your eye and then reproduced it with crayons or watercolor paints. A decade later, a public speaker discussing social injustice or environmental issues may have galvanized you into joining a charitable organization or a local cleanup project. A halftime speech by your team's coach may have spurred you and your teammates to victory, while a sermon delivered by a member of the clergy might have caused you to examine your life and faith. And at any time in your life when a disappointment or major tragedy in your life got you down, a line from a poem or song gave your spirits the lift they so desperately needed.

The beauty and the benefit of inspiration is that you become motivated to do something that will improve your life—and often the lives of others as well—in some fashion. Self-examination, whether a moment of reflection or an extended internal debate, leads to changes that produce intellectual, emotional, or physical improvement, and sometimes all three.

The source of the inspiration need not be memorable eloquence or rhetoric from the likes of John Kennedy, Dr. Martin Luther King, Helen Keller, or Sir Winston Churchill. A few words, a line of poetry, or even a fortune-cookie proverb will suffice so long as it strikes a responsive and energizing chord. Some quotations are just a few words, while some poems are reproduced in their entirety because the message is too important or too poignant to be abridged.

In that regard, this book contains inspirational writing and utterances from a variety of sources, from well-known figures to people of whom most of us have never heard. They come from all over the globe because no one culture has a monopoly on wisdom.

The lives of everyone on this planet are works in progress, so please consider this volume to be a workbook. Read an entry in light of whether it speaks to you, and if it does, contemplate how its application can be translated into action. If a friend or relative needs emotional or spiritual help, find something that you can share with him or her. Readers whose professions call on them to offer motivation or solace will also find in these pages wisdom to share.

Good luck with your lifelong work in progress, and may the contents of this book help you along the way.

Steven D. Price

2017

Chapter

· · · · · · · · · · · · ·

I

On Living a Good Life . . .
and a Better One

Yesterday is but a dream, tomorrow but a vision. But today well lived
makes every yesterday a dream of happiness, and every
tomorrow a vision of hope. Look well, therefore, to this day.
Such is the salutation to the dawn.
— SANSKRIT PROVERB

However long your stay on this small planet lasts, and whatever
happens during it, the most important thing is that—
from time to time—you feel life's sweet caress.
— JEAN BAPTISTE CHARBONNEAU

Happiness depends upon ourselves.
— ARISTOTLE

A man can do only what a man can do. But if he does that each day he
can sleep at night and do it again the next day.
— ALBERT SCHWEITZER

No need to hurry. No need to sparkle.

No need to be anybody but oneself.

—VIRGINIA WOOLF

•

May you live every day of your life.

—JONATHAN SWIFT

•

We can only be said to be alive in those moments

when our hearts are conscious of our treasures.

—THORNTON WILDER

•

Today is the first day of the rest of your life.

—SOURCE UNKNOWN

•

So whatever you want to do, just do it. . . . Making a damn fool of

yourself is absolutely essential.

—GLORIA STEINEM

With every rising of the sun

Think of your life as just begun.

—ELLA WHEELER WILCOX

•

The ideals which have lighted my way, and time after time

have given me new courage to face life cheerfully,

have been Kindness, Beauty, and Truth.

—ALBERT EINSTEIN

•

When odds are one in a million, be that one.

—SOURCE UNKNOWN

•

One cannot reflect in streaming water.

Only those who know internal peace can give it to others.

—LAO TZU

•

Live your life so that whatever you lose, you are ahead.

—CHARLES B. REEVES JR.

He is a sane man who can have tragedy in his heart and
comedy in his head.
—G. K. CHESTERTON

•

The quality, not the longevity, of one's life is what is important.
—MARTIN LUTHER KING JR.

•

He was born with a gift of laughter and a sense that the world was mad.
—RAPHAEL SABATINI

•

If I am not for myself, who will be for me?
If I am not for others, what am I?
And if not now, when?
—HILLEL THE ELDER

•

Life is made up of a series of judgments on insufficient data, and
if we waited to run down all our doubts, it would flow past us.
—LEARNED HAND

Mere longevity is a good thing for those who watch Life from the sidelines. For those who play the game, an hour may be a year, a single day's work an achievement for eternity.

—**GABRIEL HEATTER**

Life was meant to be lived, and curiosity must be kept alive. One must never, for whatever reason, turn his back on life.

—**ELEANOR ROOSEVELT**

The highest of wisdom is continual cheerfulness: such a state, like the region above the moon, is always clear and serene.

—**MICHEL DE MONTAIGNE**

Enjoy the little things in life. . . . For one day you'll look back and realize they were the big things.

—**KURT VONNEGUT**

Focusing your life solely on making a buck shows a certain
poverty of ambition. It asks too little of yourself.
Because it's only when you hitch your wagon to something
larger than yourself that you realize your true potential.
—BARACK OBAMA

•

Do not forget that the value and interest of life is not so much to do
conspicuous things . . . as to do ordinary things with the
perception of their enormous value.
—PIERRE TEILHARD DE CHARDIN

•

The three stages of a satisfying life: (1) learn, (2) earn, (3) return.
—SOURCE UNKNOWN

•

A good head and a good heart are always a formidable combination.
—NELSON MANDELA

Develop an interest in life as you see it; the people, things, literature, music—the world is so rich, simply throbbing with rich treasures, beautiful souls, and interesting people. Forget yourself.
—HENRY MILLER

•

I love the man that can smile in trouble, that can gather strength from distress, and grow brave by reflection.
—THOMAS PAINE

•

The opposite of love is not hate, it's indifference.
The opposite of art is not ugliness, it's indifference.
The opposite of faith is not heresy, it's indifference.
And the opposite of life is not death, it's indifference.
—ELIE WIESEL

•

I am an optimist. It does not seem too much use being anything else.
—SIR WINSTON CHURCHILL

To live is to choose. But to choose well, you must know who you are
and what you stand for, where you want to go and
why you want to get there.
—KOFI ANNAN

Birds sing after a storm; why shouldn't people feel as free to
delight in whatever remains to them?
—ROSE F. KENNEDY

Only put off until tomorrow what you are willing to
die having left undone.
—PABLO PICASSO

And, above all things, never think that you're not good enough
yourself. A man should never think that. My belief is that in life
people will take you very much at your own reckoning.
—ANTHONY TROLLOPE

Laughter is an instant vacation.
—MILTON BERLE

It's better to wear out than to rust out.
—AMERICAN PROVERB

•

To be astonished is one of the surest ways of
not growing old too quickly.
—SIDONIE-GABRIELLE COLETTE

•

Don't ever mistake my silence for ignorance, my calmness for
acceptance, or my kindness for weakness.
—SOURCE UNKNOWN

•

A tree is known by its fruit; a man by his deeds.
A good seed is never lost; he who sows courtesy reaps friendship, and
he who plants kindness gathers love.
—SAINT BASIL

•

Many persons have a wrong idea of what constitutes true happiness.
It is not attained through self-gratification but through fidelity to a
worthy purpose.
—HELEN KELLER

Success is getting what you want; happiness is wanting what you get.
—**DALE CARNEGIE**

❋

Many people excuse their own faults but judge other persons harshly.
We should reverse this attitude by excusing others' shortcomings
and by harshly examining our own.
—**PARAMAHANSA YOGANANDA**

❋

Even if you are on the right track, you will get run over if you just sit
there.
—**WILL ROGERS**

❋

We must be willing to let go of the life we have planned,
so as to have the life that is waiting for us.
—**E. M. FORSTER**

❋

You should never be ashamed to admit you have been wrong.
It only proves you are wiser today than yesterday.
—**JONATHAN SWIFT**

If you can't see anything beautiful about yourself, get a better mirror.
—SHANE KOYCZAN

●

You are not useless. You are not hopeless. And no matter how scared you are, you will never be alone. And deep down, somewhere, in the part of you that decided the good days and your happiness and your health were all worth fighting for, you know that, too. Hold onto that knowledge. It will see you through the worst.
—ELLA CERON

●

Nobody holds a good opinion of a man
who holds a low opinion of himself.
—ANTHONY TROLLOPE

●

The best people possess a feeling for beauty, the courage to take risks, the discipline to tell the truth, the capacity for sacrifice. Ironically, their virtues make them vulnerable; they are often wounded, sometimes destroyed.
—ERNEST HEMINGWAY

Can you remember who you were before the world

told you who you should be?

—**DANIELLE LAPORTE**

•

Keep your thoughts positive because your thoughts become your words.

Keep your words positive because your words become your behavior.

Keep your behavior positive because your behavior becomes your

habits. Keep your habits positive because your habits become your

values. Keep your values positive because your values become your

destiny.

—**MOHANDAS GANDHI**

•

You must not abandon the ship in a storm because you cannot

control the winds. . . . What you cannot turn to good,

you must at least make as little bad as you can.

—**SIR THOMAS MORE**

•

On matters of style, swim with the current, on matters of principle,

stand like a rock.

—**THOMAS JEFFERSON**

Your time is limited, don't waste it living someone else's life. Don't be trapped by dogma, which is living the result of other people's thinking. Don't let the noise of other's opinion drown your own inner voice. And most important, have the courage to follow your heart and intuition, they somehow already know what you truly want to become. Everything else is secondary.
—STEVE JOBS

You are not here merely to make a living. You are here in order to enable the world to live more amply, with greater vision, with a finer spirit of hope and achievement. You are here to enrich the world, and you impoverish yourself if you forget the errand.
—WOODROW WILSON

Man is not the sum of what he has but the totality of what he does not yet have, of what he might have.
—JEAN-PAUL SARTRE

Life is so unlike theory.
—ANTHONY TROLLOPE

Things turn out best for the people who make the
best of the way things turn out.
— ATTRIBUTED TO AN UNNAMED SOURCE

The best way to predict your future is to create it.
—ABRAHAM LINCOLN

There is no passion to be found playing small—in settling for a life that
is less than the one you are capable of living.
—NELSON MANDELA

If wrinkles must be written on our brow, let them not be written on
our heart. The spirit should never grow old.
—JAMES GARFIELD

Your example is far more influential and inspiring than any words of
instruction, or threats, or even words of encouragement.
—JONATHAN LOCKWOOD HUIE

Don't judge each day by the harvest you reap

but by the seeds that you plant.

—ROBERT LOUIS STEVENSON

•

The journey is the reward.

—CHINESE PROVERB

•

Whatever you can do, or dream you can do, begin it. Boldness has

genius, power, and magic in it. Begin it now.

—JOHANN WOLFGANG VON GOETHE

•

If you hear a voice within you saying "you cannot paint," then by all

means paint, and that voice will be silenced.

—VINCENT VAN GOGH

•

The final wisdom of life requires not the annulment

of incongruity but the achievement of serenity within and above it.

—REINHOLD NIEBUHR

When one door closes, another opens; but we often look so long and

so regretfully upon the closed door that we do not see

the one which has opened for us.

—ALEXANDER GRAHAM BELL

Great lives never go out; they go on.

—BENJAMIN HARRISON

Life is like riding a bicycle, in order to keep your balance,

you must keep moving.

—ALBERT EINSTEIN

You're off to Great Places!

Today is your day!

Your mountain is waiting,

So . . . get on your way!

—DR. SEUSS (THEODORE GEISEL)

Life is what happens to you while you're busy making other plans.

—JOHN LENNON

Thousands of candles can be lighted from a single candle, and
the life of the candle will not be shortened.
Happiness never decreases by being shared.
—BUDDHA

•

We must always change, renew, rejuvenate ourselves;
otherwise we harden.
—JOHANN WOLFGANG VON GOETHE

•

The purpose of life is to live it, to taste experience to the utmost, to
reach out eagerly and without fear for newer and richer experience.
—ELEANOR ROOSEVELT

•

The best time to plant a tree was twenty years ago. The second best
time is now.
—CHINESE PROVERB

•

An unexamined life is not worth living.
—SOCRATES

I have never been hurt by what I have not said.
—**CALVIN COOLIDGE**

＊

Worry never robs tomorrow of its sorrow, it only saps today of its joy.
—**LEO BUSCAGLIA**

＊

A difficult time can be more readily endured if we retain the conviction that our existence holds a purpose—a cause to pursue, a person to love, a goal to achieve.
—**JOHN MAXWELL**

＊

Dream as if you'll live forever, live as if you'll die today.
—**JAMES DEAN**

＊

For the man who prays in his heart, the whole world is a church.
—**SYLVAIN OF ATHOS**

＊

He who lives in harmony with himself lives in harmony with the universe.
—**MARCUS AURELIUS**

Your worst enemy cannot harm you as much as
your own unguarded thoughts.
—BUDDHA

If you have great challenges, have greater faith.
—LEINANI KAMAKA

Man is an instrument. His life is the melody.
—YIDDISH PROVERB

You pray in your distress and in your need. Would that you might pray
also in the fullness of your joy and in your days of abundance.
—KAHLIL GIBRAN

Preach the Gospel, and if necessary use words.
—SOURCE UNKNOWN

Life must be lived forwards, but can only be understood backwards.
—SØREN KIERKEGAARD

Great souls have wills, feeble ones have only wishes.

—CHINESE PROVERB

God grant me the serenity

to accept the things I cannot change;

the courage to change the things I can;

and the wisdom to know the difference.

—REINHOLD NIEBUHR

(TO WHOM THIS SERENITY PRAYER IS ATTRIBUTED)

Good humor is a tonic for mind and body.

It is the best antidote for anxiety and depression.

It is a business asset.

It attracts and keeps friends.

It lightens human burdens.

It is the direct route to serenity and contentment.

—GRENVILLE KLEISER

Peace . . . is a condition of mind brought about by a serenity of soul.
Peace is not merely the absence of war. It is also a state of mind.
Lasting peace can come only to peaceful people.

—JAWAHARLAL NEHRU

Curiosity endows the people who have it with a generosity in argument
and a serenity in their own mode of life which springs from their
cheerful willingness to let life take the form it will.

—ALISTAIR COOKE

When I want to think, I sit. When I want to change, I act.

—JAPANESE PROVERB

Coolness and absence of heat and haste indicate fine qualities.

—RALPH WALDO EMERSON

Serenity is knowing that your worst shot is still pretty good.

—JOHNNY MILLER

The future belongs to those who believe in the beauty of their dreams.
—ELEANOR ROOSEVELT

●

I shall live this day as if it is my last. And if it is not,

I shall fall to my knees and give thanks.
—OG MANDINO

●

Sow a thought, and you reap an act; sow an act, and you reap a habit;

sow a habit, and you reap a character; sow a character,

and you reap a destiny.
—CHARLES READE

●

Character cannot be developed in ease and quiet. Only through

experiences of trial and suffering can the soul be strengthened, vision

cleared, ambition inspired, and success achieved.
—HELEN KELLER

●

Don't cry when the sun is gone,

because the tears won't let you see the stars.
—VIOLETA PARRA

Don't go through life, grow through life.
—ERIC BUTTERWORTH

•

By trying, you may fail others. By not, you fail yourself.
—SOURCE UNKNOWN

•

Things work out best for those who make the best
of how things work out.
—JOHN WOODEN

•

Many people become bankrupt through having invested too heavily in
the prose of life. To have ruined one's self over poetry is an honor.
—OSCAR WILDE

If the soul is left in darkness, sins will be committed. The guilty one is
not he who commits the sin, but the one who causes the darkness.
—**TAVIS SMILEY**

Every man is guilty of all the good he did not do.
—**VOLTAIRE**

If the only prayer you ever say in your entire life is
"Thank You," it will be enough.
—**MEISTER ECKHART**

Be patient and calm; no one can catch a fish with anger.
—**HERBERT HOOVER**

Damaged people are dangerous. They know they can survive.
—**JOSEPHINE HART**

The minute you settle for less than you deserve,

you get even less than you settled for.

—**MAUREEN DOWD**

•

You were given this life because you were strong enough to live it.

—**SOURCE UNKNOWN**

•

In the end, we will remember not the words of our enemies,

but the silence of our friends.

—**MARTIN LUTHER KING JR.**

•

Better to light one small candle / than to curse the darkness.

—**CHINESE PROVERB**

•

And you would accept the seasons of your heart just as you have always

accepted that seasons pass over your fields and you would watch with

serenity through the winters of your grief.

—**KAHLIL GIBRAN**

Despair is the damp of hell, as joy is the serenity of heaven.
—JOHN DONNE

The trouble with most of us is that we would rather
be ruined by praise than saved by criticism.
—NORMAN VINCENT PEALE

Boredom is the feeling that everything is a waste of time;
serenity, that nothing is.
—THOMAS SZASZ

What I dream of is an art of balance, of purity and serenity devoid
of troubling or depressing subject matter . . . a soothing, calming
influence on the mind, rather like a good armchair which provides
relaxation from physical fatigue.
—HENRI MATISSE

Be who you are and say what you feel because those who mind don't
matter and those who matter don't mind.
—DR. SEUSS [THEODORE GEISEL]

Time spent laughing is time spent with the gods.
—**JAPANESE PROVERB**

People will forget what you said, people will forget what you did,

but people will never forget how you made them feel.
—**MAYA ANGELOU**

What lies behind us and what lies before us are tiny matters compared

to what lies within us.
—**OLIVER WENDELL HOLMES**

Hitch your wagon to a star.
—**RALPH WALDO EMERSON**

Happiness is when what you think, what you say,

and what you do are in harmony.
—**MOHANDAS GANDHI**

Regret for wasted time is more wasted time.
—**MASON COOLEY**

Don't ask "Why"; ask instead, "Why not."
—**JOHN F. KENNEDY**

The important work of moving the world forward does not wait to be done by perfect men.
—**GEORGE ELIOT**

The greatest mistake you can make in life is to be continually fearing you will make one.
—**ELBERT HUBBARD**

A man is not old until his regrets take the place of his dreams.
—**YIDDISH PROVERB**

If you wish to experience peace, provide peace for another.
—**TENZIN GYATSO, THE FOURTEENTH DALAI LAMA**

A pessimist sees the difficulty in every opportunity;

an optimist sees the opportunity in every difficulty.

—SIR WINSTON CHURCHILL

•

We don't stop playing because we grow old;

we grow old because we stop playing.

—GEORGE BERNARD SHAW

•

My mission in life is not merely to survive, but to thrive; and to do so

with some passion, some compassion, some humor, and some style.

—MAYA ANGELOU

•

If you are patient in one moment of anger,

you will escape a hundred days of sorrow.

—CHINESE PROVERB

Twenty years from now you will be more disappointed by the
things you didn't do than by the ones you did do. So throw off the
bowlines. Sail away from the safe harbor. Catch the trade winds
in your sails. Explore. Dream. Discover.

—ATTRIBUTED TO MARK TWAIN

Finish each day and be done with it. You have done what you could.
Some blunders and absurdities no doubt crept in; forget them as soon
as you can. Tomorrow is a new day; begin it well and serenely and with
too high a spirit to be encumbered with your old nonsense.

—RALPH WALDO EMERSON

If you can talk with crowds and keep your virtue,
Or walk with Kings—nor lose the common touch,
If neither foes nor loving friends can hurt you,
If all men count with you, but none too much:
If you can fill the unforgiving minute
With sixty seconds' worth of distance run,
Yours is the Earth and everything that's in it,
And—which is more—you'll be a Man, my son!

—RUDYARD KIPLING

Spend all you have for loveliness,

Buy it and never count the cost;

For one white singing hour of peace

Count many a year of strife well lost,

And for a breath of ecstasy

Give all you have been, or could be.

—SARA TEASDALE

Happy the man, and happy he alone,

He who can call today his own:

He who, secure within, can say,

Tomorrow do thy worst, for I have lived today.

Be fair or foul or rain or shine

The joys I have possessed, in spite of fate, are mine.

Not Heaven itself upon the past has power,

But what has been, has been, and I have had my hour.

—JOHN DRYDEN, TRANSLATION OF HORACE

Chapter

· · · · · · · · · · ·

II

On Sharing with Others

Youth ends when egotism does;

maturity begins when one lives for others.

—HERMANN HESSE

•

Love for other people what you love for yourself.

—ISLAMIC PROVERB

•

Never measure your generosity by what you give,

but rather by what you have left.

—BISHOP FULTON J. SHEEN

•

Those who bring sunshine to the lives of others

cannot keep it from themselves.

—SIR JAMES M. BARRIE

•

But it is impossible to go through life without trust; that is to be

imprisoned in the worst cell of all, oneself.

—GRAHAM GREENE

The wise man does not lay up his own treasures.

The more he gives to others, the more he has for his own.

—LAO TZU

❀

The longer we live, the more we find we are like other persons.

—OLIVER WENDELL HOLMES SR.

❀

A generous heart, kind speech, and a life of service and compassion

are the things which renew humanity.

—BUDDHA

❀

I've learned that you shouldn't go through life with a catcher's mitt on

both hands. You need to be able to throw something back.

—MAYA ANGELOU

❀

Do not judge another until you have walked two moons in his

moccasins.

—NATIVE AMERICAN PROVERB

The best way to find yourself is to lose yourself in the service of others.
—**MOHANDAS GANDHI**

Try not to become a man of success, but rather to become a man of value. He is considered successful in our day who gets more out of life than he puts in. But a man of value will give more than he receives.
—**ALBERT EINSTEIN**

Keep away from people who try to belittle your ambitions.
Small people always do that, but the really great
make you feel that you, too, can become great.
—**MARK TWAIN**

Logic will get you from A to B. Imagination will take you everywhere.
—**ALBERT EINSTEIN**

Never doubt that a small group of thoughtful, committed citizens can change the world. Indeed, it is the only thing that ever has.
—**MARGARET MEAD**

The next best thing to being wise oneself is to

live in a circle of those who are.

—C. S. LEWIS

At last you are no longer searching for yourself, but for another—

you are saved.

—JEAN GIRAUDOUX

The true measure of a man is how he treats someone

who can do him absolutely no good.

—ANN LANDERS

It is when we try to grapple with another man's intimate need that we

perceive how incomprehensible, wavering, and misty are the beings

that share with us the sight of the stars and the warmth of the sun.

—JOSEPH CONRAD

As you grow older you will discover that you have two hands.

One for helping yourself, the other for helping others.

—AUDREY HEPBURN

We make a living by what we get. We make a life by what we give.
—SIR WINSTON CHURCHILL

How far you go in life depends on your being tender with the young,
compassionate with the aged, sympathetic with the striving and
tolerant of the weak and the strong. Because someday in life you
will have been all of these.
—GEORGE WASHINGTON CARVER

You're only here for a short visit. Don't hurry, don't worry.
And be sure to smell the flowers along the way.
—WALTER HAGEN

None knows the weight of another's burden.
—THOMAS FULLER

Life is an exciting business, and most exciting when
it is lived for others.
—HELEN KELLER

Man is a knot, a web, a mesh into which relationships are tied.

Only those relationships matter

—ANTOINE DE SAINT-EXUPÉRY

If you want happiness for an hour, take a nap. If you want happiness for

a day, go fishing. If you want happiness for a month, get married.

If you want happiness for a year, inherit a fortune. If you want

happiness for a lifetime, help someone else.

—CHINESE PROVERB

One learns peoples through the heart, not the eyes or the intellect.

—MARK TWAIN

The full measure of a man is not to be found in the man himself,

but in the colors and textures that come alive in others because of him.

—ALBERT SCHWEITZER

Do not hear one and judge two.

—GREEK PROVERB

If you judge people, you have not time to love them.
—MOTHER TERESA

*

As we grow as unique persons,

we learn to respect the uniqueness of others.
—REV. ROBERT H. SCHULLER

*

Forgiveness is a way of opening up the doors again and moving

forward, whether it's a personal life or a national life.
—HILLARY RODHAM CLINTON

*

One of the sanest, surest, and most generous joys of life

comes from being happy over the good fortune of others.
—ROBERT A. HEINLEIN

*

Whoever walks with the wise becomes wise,

but the companion of fools will suffer harm.
—PROVERBS 13:20

Hate is never conquered by hate,

Hate is only conquered by love.

— BUDDHA

•

Life has got a habit of not standing hitched. You got to ride it like you find it. You got to change with it. If a day goes by that don't change some of your old notions for new ones, that is just about like trying to milk a dead cow.

— WOODY GUTHRIE

•

Don't build your happiness on someone else's unhappiness.

— RICHARD ROSE

•

If you want to lift yourself up, lift up someone else.

— BOOKER T. WASHINGTON

•

Do not judge, and you will never be mistaken.

— JEAN-JACQUES ROUSSEAU

Life is not a spectator sport. If you're going to spend your
whole life in the grandstand just watching what goes on,
in my opinion you're wasting your life.
— **JACKIE ROBINSON**

•

Be kind, for everyone you meet is fighting a harder battle.
— **PLATO**

•

Love and work are the cornerstones of our humanness.
— **SIGMUND FREUD**

•

What you leave behind is not what is engraved in stone monuments,
but what is woven into the lives of others.
— **PERICLES**

•

The first thing to learn in intercourse with others is non-interference
with their own particular ways of being happy, provided those ways
do not assume to interfere by violence with ours.
— **WILLIAM JAMES**

Be glad, and your friends are many;

Be sad, and you lose them all,

There are none to decline your nectared wine,

But alone you must drink life's gall.

—ELLA WHEELER WILCOX

*

If I can stop one heart from breaking,

I shall not live in vain;

If I can ease one life the aching,

Or cool one pain,

Or help one fainting robin

Unto his nest again,

I shall not live in vain.

—EMILY DICKINSON

No man is an island,

Entire of itself,

Every man is a piece of the continent,

A part of the main.

If a clod be washed away by the sea,

Europe is the less.

As well as if a promontory were.

As well as if a manor of thy friend's

Or of thine own were:

Any man's death diminishes me,

Because I am involved in mankind,

And therefore never send to know for whom the bell tolls;

It tolls for thee.

—JOHN DONNE

Chapter

· · · · · · · · · · ·

III

On Success

Success consists of going from failure to failure without
loss of enthusiasm.
—SIR WINSTON CHURCHILL

The person who gets the farthest is generally the one who is willing to
do and dare. The sure-thing boat never gets far from shore.
—DALE CARNEGIE

When people tell me they've learned from experience,
I tell them the trick is to learn from other people's experience.
—WARREN BUFFETT

Coming together is a beginning; keeping together is progress;
working together is success.
—HENRY FORD

Genius is one percent inspiration and ninety-nine percent perspiration.
—THOMAS EDISON

I know the price of success: dedication, hard work, and an unremitting devotion to the things you want to see happen.

—**FRANK LLOYD WRIGHT**

I found that the men and women who got to the top were those who did the jobs they had in hand, with everything they had of energy and enthusiasm and hard work.

—**HARRY S. TRUMAN**

Would you like me to give you a formula for success? It's quite simple, really. Double your rate of failure. You are thinking of failure as the enemy of success. But it isn't at all. You can be discouraged by failure or you can learn from it, so go ahead and make mistakes. Make all you can. Because remember that's where you will find success.

—**THOMAS J. WATSON**

A leader is one who knows the way, goes the way, and shows the way.

—**JOHN MAXWELL**

Don't say you don't have enough time. You have exactly the same
number of hours per day that were given to Helen Keller,
Pasteur, Michelangelo, Mother Teresa, Leonardo da Vinci,
Thomas Jefferson, and Albert Einstein.
—H. JACKSON BROWN JR.

If you want your dreams to come true, don't sleep.
—YIDDISH PROVERB

Find a need and fill it.
—RUTH STAFFORD PEALE

After climbing a great hill,
one only finds that there are many more hills to climb.
—NELSON MANDELA

Most people give up just when they're about to achieve success.
They quit on the one-yard line. They give up at the last minute
of the game, one foot from a winning touchdown.
—H. ROSS PEROT

The man who removes a mountain begins by carrying away small stones.
—CHINESE PROVERB

Aim for success, not perfection. Never give up your right to be wrong, because then you will lose the ability to learn new things and move forward with your life. Remember that fear always lurks behind perfectionism.
—DAVID M. BURNS

Only those who will risk going too far can possibly find out how far one can go.
—T. S. ELIOT

Many hands make light work.
—ENGLISH PROVERB

Failure is success if we learn from it.
—MALCOLM FORBES

The man who will use his skill and constructive imagination to see how much he can give for a dollar, instead of how little he can give for a dollar, is bound to succeed.

—HENRY FORD

The secret of success is constancy to purpose.

—BENJAMIN FRANKLIN

Good is not good where better is expected.

—THOMAS FULLER

No one can possibly achieve any real and lasting success or get rich in business by being a conformist.

—J. PAUL GETTY

Vision without action is daydream. Action without vision is nightmare.

—JAPANESE PROVERB

Successful men are influenced by the desire for pleasing results. Failures are influenced by the desire for pleasing methods and are inclined to be satisfied with such results as can be obtained by doing things they like to do. The common denominator of success—the secret of every man who has ever been successful—lies in the fact that he formed the habit of doing things that failures don't like to do.

—ALBERT E. N. GRAY

•

Men give me credit for some genius. All the genius I have lies in this: when I have a subject in hand, I study it profoundly. Day and night it is before me. I explore it in all its bearings. My mind becomes pervaded with it. Then the effort which I have made is what people are pleased to call the fruit of genius. It is the fruit of labor and thought.

—ALEXANDER HAMILTON

•

Personal development is your springboard to personal excellence. Ongoing, continuous, non-stop personal development literally assures you that there is no limit to what you can accomplish.

—BRIAN TRACY

Many people allow their need for other people's

approval to control their lives.

They spend their lives worrying about what others think of them.

—RICK WARREN

•

Too many people overvalue what they are not,

and undervalue what they are.

—MALCOLM S. FORBES

•

Success usually comes to those who are too busy to be looking for it.

—HENRY DAVID THOREAU

•

A man can fail many times, but he isn't a failure until he begins to

blame somebody else.

—JOHN BURROUGHS

•

Knowing is not enough; we must apply.

Willing is not enough; we must do.

—JOHANN WOLFGANG VON GOETHE

I do not think there is any other quality so essential to
success of any kind as the quality of perseverance.
It overcomes almost everything, even nature.
—JOHN D. ROCKEFELLER

I have learned that success is to be measured not so much by the
position that one has reached in life as by the obstacles which
he has overcome while trying to succeed.
—BOOKER T. WASHINGTON

Take the pains required to become what you want to become, or
you might end up becoming something you'd rather not be.
That is also a daily discipline and worth considering.
—DONALD J. TRUMP

It is better to aim at perfection and miss it
than to aim at imperfection and hit it.
—THOMAS WATSON

The older I get, the more I see a straight path where I want to go.
If you're going to hunt elephants, don't get off the trail for a rabbit.
—T. BOONE PICKENS

Success is not about doing things well or even very well, or being
acknowledged by others. It is not an external opinion, but rather an
internal status. It is the harmony between the soul and your emotions,
which requires love, family, friendship, authenticity and integrity.
—CARLOS SLIM HELÚ

I believe the true road to preeminent success in any line is to make
yourself master in that line. I have no faith in the policy of scattering
one's resources, and in my experience I have rarely if ever met a man
who achieved preeminence in money making—certainly never one in
manufacturing—who was interested in many concerns.
—ANDREW CARNEGIE

Success is often achieved by those who don't know
that failure is inevitable.
—COCO CHANEL

No man can climb the ladder of success without first

placing his foot on the bottom rung.

—JAMES CASH PENNY

Fortune sides with him who dares.

—VIRGIL

The successful person has the habit of doing the things

failures don't like to do.

—ALBERT E. N. GRAY

The size of your success is measured by the strength of your desire, the

size of your dream, and how you handle disappointment along the way.

—ROBERT KIYOSAKI

To do a common thing uncommonly well brings success.

—HENRY J. HEINZ

The successful team is the one that makes 1 plus 1 equal 11.
—SHEIK MOHAMMED BIN RASHID AL MAKTOUM

The man who has done his level best, and who is conscious that
he has done his best, is a success, even though the world may
write him down as a failure.
—BERTIE CHARLES FORBES

I like thinking big. If you're going to be thinking anything,
you might as well think big.
—DONALD J. TRUMP

There is no royal flower-strewn path to success. And if there is,
I have not found it for if I have accomplished anything in life
it is because I have been willing to work hard.
—MADAM C. J. WALKER

If A equal success, then the formula is A equals X plus Y and Z, with
X being work, Y play, and Z keeping your mouth shut.
—ALBERT EINSTEIN

The most successful businessman is the man who holds onto the old just as long as it is good, and grabs the new just as soon as it is better.
—LEE IACOCCA

My success wasn't based on how I could push down everyone around me. My success was based on how much I could push everybody up . . . And in the process they pushed me up, and I pushed them up, and we kept doing that, and we still do that.
—GEORGE LUCAS

If a man write a better book, preach a better sermon, or make a better mouse-trap than his neighbor, tho' he build his house in the woods, the world will make a beaten path to his door.
—RALPH WALDO EMERSON

Look up at the stars and not down at your feet.
Try to make sense of what you see, and wonder about what makes the universe exist. Be curious.
—STEPHEN HAWKING

The secret of my success is a two-word answer: Know people.
— **HARVEY S. FIRESTONE**

•

The secret of success is to do common things uncommonly well.
— **JOHN D. ROCKEFELLER**

•

Criticism may not be agreeable, but it is necessary.
It fulfills the same function as pain in the human body.
It calls attention to an unhealthy state of things.
— **SIR WINSTON CHURCHILL**

•

My method was deliberate, and simple, and drastic. In the first place,
I resolved to do my work, no matter how hard or dangerous it might
be, so well that no man would be called upon to do it for me.
Further, I put ginger in my muscles.
— **JACK LONDON**

•

Everyone who got where he is has had to begin where he was.
— **ROBERT LOUIS STEVENSON**

A non-doer is very often a critic—that is, someone who
sits back and watches doers, and then waxes philosophically about
how the doers are doing. It's easy to be a critic, but
being a doer requires effort, risk, and change.

—DR. WAYNE DYER

Do not be desirous of having things done quickly. Do not look at small
advantages. Desire to have things done quickly prevents their being
done thoroughly. Looking at small advantages prevents great affairs
from being accomplished.

—CONFUCIUS

The greater the difficulty, the more glory in surmounting it.
Skillful pilots gain their reputation from storms and tempests.

—EPICTETUS

We live in deeds, not years: In thoughts not breaths; in feelings, not in
figures on a dial. We should count time by heartthrobs. He most lives
who thinks most, feels the noblest, acts the best.

—DAVID BAILEY

Success is not measured by what you accomplish but by the opposition
you have encountered, and the courage with which you have
maintained the struggle against overwhelming odds.
—ORISON SWETT MARDEN

The first requisite of success is the ability to apply your physical and
mental energies to one problem without growing weary.
—THOMAS EDISON

Empty pockets never held anyone back.
Only empty heads and empty hearts can do that.
—NORMAN VINCENT PEALE

It's your aptitude, not just your attitude,
that determines your ultimate altitude.
—HILARY "ZIG" ZIGLAR

The only way around is through.
—ROBERT FROST

Great things are not done by impulse,

but by a series of small things brought together.

—VINCENT VAN GOGH

I feel that the greatest reward for doing is the opportunity to do more.

—JONAS SALK

The best job goes to the person who can get it done without

passing the buck or coming back with excuses.

—NAPOLEON HILL

Trust yourself. Create the kind of self that you will be happy to live

with all your life. Make the most of yourself by fanning the tiny,

inner sparks of possibility into flames of achievement.

—FOSTER C. MCCLELLAN

I am always doing things I can't do, that's how I get to do them.

—PABLO PICASSO

The average estimate themselves by what they do,

the above average by what they are.

—JOHANN FRIEDRICH VON SCHILLER

Young people tell what they are doing, old people what they

have done, and fools what they wish to do.

—FRENCH PROVERB

The man who wakes up and finds himself famous hasn't been asleep.

—SOURCE UNKNOWN

Nothing splendid has ever been achieved except by those who dared

believe that something inside them was superior to circumstances.

—BRUCE BARTON

The biggest adventure you can ever take is to

live the life of your dreams.

—OPRAH WINFREY

No bird soars too high if he soars with his own wings.
— **WILLIAM BLAKE**

Destiny is not a matter of chance, it is a matter of choice;
it is not a thing to be waited for, it is a thing to be achieved.
— **WILLIAM JENNINGS BRYAN**

This became a credo of mine . . . attempt the impossible
in order to improve your work.
— **BETTE DAVIS**

Unless a man undertakes more than he possibly can do,
he will never do all that he can.
— **HENRY DRUMMOND**

Hell, there are no rules here —we're trying to accomplish something.
— **THOMAS ALVA EDISON**

We succeed only as we identify in life, or in war, or in anything else,
a single overriding objective, and make all other considerations
bend to that one objective.
—DWIGHT D. EISENHOWER

•

What is the recipe for successful achievement? To my mind there
are just four essential ingredients: Choose a career you love. . . .
Give it the best there is in you. . . . Seize your opportunities.
And be a member of the team. In no country but America,
I believe, is it possible to fulfill all four of these requirements.
—BENJAMIN F. FAIRLESS

•

A successful man continues to look for work after he has found a job.
—SOURCE UNKNOWN

•

To understand the heart and mind of a person, look not at what he has
already achieved, but at what he aspires to.
—KAHLIL GIBRAN

Get going. Move forward. Aim high. Plan a takeoff. Don't just sit on the runway and hope someone will come along and push the airplane. It simply won't happen. Change your attitude and gain some altitude. Believe me, you'll love it up here.

—**DONALD J. TRUMP**

A man is a success if he gets up in the morning and gets to bed at night, and in between he does what he wants to do.

—**BOB DYLAN**

I make progress by having people around me who are smarter than I am and listening to them. And I assume that everyone is smarter about something than I am.

—**HENRY J. KAISER**

Never measure the height of a mountain, until you have reached the top. Then you will see how low it was.

—**DAG HAMMARSKJÖLD**

My mother drew a distinction between achievement and success.
She said that achievement is the knowledge that you have studied and
worked hard and done the best that is in you. Success is being praised
by others. That is nice but not as important or satisfying.
Always aim for achievement and forget about success.
—HELEN HAYES

•

We are more ready to try the untried when what we do is
inconsequential. Hence the remarkable fact that many inventions had
their birth as toys.
—ERIC HOFFER

•

Decide what you want, decide what you are willing to exchange for it.
Establish your priorities and go to work.
—H. L. HUNT

•

Only those who dare to fail greatly can ever achieve greatly.
—ROBERT F. KENNEDY

It is time for us all to stand and cheer for the doer, the achiever—
the one who recognizes the challenge and does something about it.
—**VINCE LOMBARDI**

Hell begins on the day when God grants us a clear vision of all that we
might have achieved, of all the gifts which we might have wasted,
of all that we might have done which we did not do.
—**GIAN CARLO MENOTTI**

Someone has defined genius as intensity of purpose: the ability to do,
the patience to wait. . . . Put these together and you have genius,
and you have achievement.
—**LEO J. MUIR**

Achievement is largely the product of steadily raising one's
levels of aspiration . . . and expectation.
—**JACK NICKLAUS**

Never tell people how to do things. Tell them what to do and
they will surprise you with their ingenuity.
—**GEN. GEORGE S. PATTON JR.**

•

Five minutes, just before going to sleep, given to a bit of directed
imagination regarding achievement possibilities of the morrow, will
steadily and increasingly bear fruit, particularly if all ideas of difficulty,
worry, or fear are resolutely ruled out and replaced by those of
accomplishment and smiling courage.
—**FREDERICK PIERCE**

•

The harder you fall, the higher you bounce.
—**SOURCE UNKNOWN**

•

Competition is a by-product of productive work, not its goal.
A creative man is motivated by the desire to achieve,
not by the desire to beat others.
—**AYN RAND**

There are only two roads that lead to something like human happiness.

They are marked by the words . . . love and achievement. . . .

In order to be happy oneself it is necessary to make at least one

other person happy. . . . The secret of human happiness is

not in self-seeking but in self-forgetting.

—**DR. THEODOR REIK**

Winner's Blueprint for Achievement:

BELIEVE while others are doubting.

PLAN while others are playing.

STUDY while others are sleeping.

DECIDE while others are delaying.

PREPARE while others are daydreaming.

BEGIN while others are procrastinating.

WORK while others are wishing.

SAVE while others are wasting.

LISTEN while others are talking.

SMILE while others are frowning.

Kids go where there is excitement. They stay where there is love.

COMMEND while others are criticizing.

PERSIST while others are quitting.

—**WILLIAM ARTHUR WARD**

Periods of tranquility are seldom prolific of creative achievement.
Mankind has to be stirred up.
—ALFRED NORTH WHITEHEAD

Do not let what you cannot do interfere with what you can do.
—JOHN WOODEN

Achievement seems to be connected with action. Successful men and
women keep moving. They make mistakes, but they don't quit.
—CONRAD HILTON

Most successful men have not achieved their distinction by having
some new talent or opportunity presented to them. They have
developed the opportunity that was at hand.
—BRUCE BARTON

When a man feels throbbing within him the power to do what he
undertakes as well as it can possibly be done, this is happiness,
this is success.
—ORISON SWETT MARDEN

Success doesn't come to you—you go to it.
— MARVA COLLINS

The difference between a successful person and others is not a lack of strength, not a lack of knowledge, but rather in a lack of will.
— VINCE LOMBARDI

Success is a journey, not a destination.
— BEN SWEETLAND

The difference between failure and success is doing a thing nearly right and doing a thing exactly right.
— EDWARD SIMMONS

No one ever attains very eminent success by simply doing what is required of him; it is the amount and excellence of what is over and above the required that determines the greatness of ultimate distinction.
— CHARLES KENDALL ADAMS

The secret of success in life is for a man to be ready

for his opportunity when it comes.

—BENJAMIN DISRAELI

My list of ingredients for success is divided into four basic groups:

Inward, Outward, Upward, and Onward.

—DAVID THOMAS

God gives every bird a worm, but he does not throw it into the nest.

—SWEDISH PROVERB

Unless you're willing to have a go, fail miserably, and

have another go, success won't happen.

—PHILLIP ADAMS

The greatest form of maturity is at harvest time. That is when we must

learn how to reap without complaint if the amounts are small and

how to reap without apology if the amounts are big.

—JIM ROHN

When a man is willing and eager, the gods join in.
— AESCHYLUS

•

Grow antennae, not horns.
— DR. JAMES ROWLAND ANGELL
(WHEN ASKED THE SECRET OF LONGEVITY AND
SUCCESS AS PRESIDENT OF YALE UNIVERSITY)

•

As you climb the ladder of success, check occasionally to make sure it
is leaning against the right wall.
— SOURCE UNKNOWN

•

The worst bankrupt in the world is the man who has lost his
enthusiasm. Let a man lose everything else in the world but his
enthusiasm and he will come through again to success.
— H. W. ARNOLD

One important key to success is self-confidence.

An important key to self-confidence is preparation.
—ARTHUR ASHE

•

The penalty for success is to be bored by the
people who used to snub you.
—LADY NANCY ASTOR

•

With time and patience, the mulberry leaf becomes satin.
—CHINESE PROVERB

•

I was made to work. If you are equally industrious,
you will be equally successful.
—JOHANN SEBASTIAN BACH

•

Whatever task you undertake, do it with all your heart and soul. . . .
Do not blame anybody for your mistakes and failures. Do not look for
approval except the consciousness of doing your best.
—BERNARD M. BARUCH

He is the best sailor who can steer within fewest points of the wind,
and exact a motive power out of the greatest obstacles.
— **SIR WALTER SCOTT**

●

The most successful men in the end are those whose success is the
result of steady accretion. . . . It is the man who carefully advances step
by step, with his mind becoming wider and wider and progressively
better able to grasp any theme or situation, persevering in what he
knows to be practical, and concentrating his thought upon it, who is
bound to succeed in the greatest degree.
— **ALEXANDER GRAHAM BELL**

●

The toughest thing about success is that you've got to keep on
being a success. Talent is only a starting point in business.
You've got to keep working that talent.
— **IRVING BERLIN**

●

Meet success like a gentleman and disaster like a man.
— **F. E. SMITH, LORD BIRKENHEAD**

The victory of success is half won when one gains the habit of work.
—SARAH KNOWLES BOLTON

•

Success is a state of mind. If you want success,

start thinking of yourself as a success.
—DR. JOYCE BROTHERS

•

The road to success is not to be run upon by seven-leagued boots.
Step by step, little by little, bit by bit—that is the way to wealth,

that is the way to wisdom, that is the way to glory.
—SIR THOMAS FOWELL BUXTON

•

The important thing to recognize is that it takes a team, and

the team ought to get credit for the wins and the losses.

Successes have many fathers, failures have none.
—PHILIP CALDWELL

Celebrate your success and find humor in your failures. Don't take yourself so seriously. Loosen up and everyone around you will loosen up. Have fun and always show enthusiasm. When all else fails, put on a costume and sing a silly song.

—SAM WALTON

Your successes and happiness are forgiven you only if you generously consent to share them.

—ALBERT CAMUS

It takes twenty years to make an overnight success.

—EDDIE CANTOR

Failure is the condiment that gives success its flavor.

—TRUMAN CAPOTE

If your actions inspire others to dream more, learn more, do more, and become more, you are a leader.

—JOHN QUINCY ADAMS

Put all your eggs in one basket and watch that basket.
—ANDREW CARNEGIE

There is but one straight road to success, and that is merit.
The man who is successful is the man who is useful.
Capacity never lacks opportunity. It cannot remain undiscovered,
because it is sought by too many anxious to use it.
—BOURKE COCKRAN

In order to succeed you must fail,
so that you know what not to do the next time.
—ANTHONY D'ANGELO

Somehow I can't believe there are many heights that can't be scaled by
a man who knows the secret of making dreams come true. This special
secret can be summarized in four Cs. They are: curiosity, confidence,
courage, and constancy, and the greatest of these is confidence.
—WALT DISNEY

The most successful people in life are generally

those who have the best information.

—BENJAMIN DISRAELI

A man is a success if he gets up in the morning and gets to bed at

night, and in between he does what he wants to do.

—BOB DYLAN

Many of life's failures are people who did not realize how close

they were to success when they gave up.

—THOMAS EDISON

Self-trust is the first secret of success.

—RALPH WALDO EMERSON

The great dividing line between success and failure can be

expressed in five words: I did not have time.

—FRANKLIN FIELD

Twelve Priceless Qualities of Success:

1. The value of time.

2. The success of perseverance.

3. The pleasure of working.

4. The dignity of simplicity.

5. The worth of character.

6. The power of kindness.

7. The influence of example.

8. The obligation of duty.

9. The wisdom of economy.

10. The virtue of patience.

11. The improvement of talent.

12. The joy of originating.

—MARSHALL FIELD

To laugh often and love much; to win the respect of intelligent persons and the affection of children; to earn the approbation of honest critics and to endure the betrayal of false friends; to appreciate beauty; to find the best in others; to give of one's self; to leave the world a little better, whether by a healthy child, a garden patch or a redeemed social condition; to have played and laughed with enthusiasm and sung with exultation; to know that even one life has breathed easier because you have lived—this is to have succeeded.

—RALPH WALDO EMERSON

Chapter

· · · · · · · · · · ·

IV

On Coping with and
Overcoming Adversity

Every great dream begins with a dreamer. Always remember,
you have within you the strength, the patience, and
the passion to reach for the stars to change the world.
—HARRIET TUBMAN

The difference between the impossible and
the possible lies in a person's determination.
—TOMMY LASORDA

You get to know who you really are in a crisis.
—OPRAH WINFREY

We either make ourselves miserable or strong.
The amount of work is the same.
—CARLOS CASTANEDA

The harder the conflict, the greater the triumph.
—GEORGE WASHINGTON

When you have a sorrow that is too great it leaves no room for any other.
EMILE ZOLA

A righteous man falls down seven times and gets up.
—PROVERBS 24:16

He that struggles with us strengthens our nerves, and
sharpens our skill. Our antagonist is our helper.
—EDMUND BURKE

There is no better than adversity. Every defeat, every heartbreak,
every loss, contains its own seed, its own lesson on how to improve
your performance next time.
—MALCOLM X

Look well into thyself; there is a source of strength which will always
spring up if thou wilt always look there.
—M. ANTONIUS

Skill and confidence are an unconquered army.
— **GEORGE HERBERT**

The measure of a man is the way he bears up under misfortune.
— **PLUTARCH**

The only one who can make you give up is yourself.
— **SIDNEY SHELDON**

Nothing in the world can take the place of persistence. Talent will not; nothing is more common than unsuccessful men with talent. Genius will not; unrewarded genius is almost a proverb. Education alone will not; the world is full of educated derelicts. Persistence and determination alone are omnipotent. The slogan "press on" has solved and always will solve the problems of the human race.
— **CALVIN COOLIDGE**

It is a shameful thing for the soul to faint while the body still perseveres.
— **MARCUS AURELIUS**

By perseverance, study, and eternal desire, any man can become great.
—GEN. GEORGE S. PATTON JR.

●

The Chinese use two brush strokes to write the word "crisis."

One brush stroke stands for danger; the other for opportunity.

In a crisis, be aware of the danger, but recognize the opportunity.
—JOHN F. KENNEDY

●

Better bread with water than cake with trouble.
—RUSSIAN PROVERB

●

Confidence comes not from always being right but

from not fearing to be wrong.
—PETER T. MCINTYRE

●

Courage is endurance for one moment more.
—UNIDENTIFIED MARINE SERVING IN VIETNAM

I am not afraid of storms, for I am learning how to sail my ship.
—**LOUISA MAY ALCOTT**

Nothing great will ever be achieved without great men, and men are great only if they are determined to be so.
—**CHARLES DE GAULLE**

If your determination is fixed, I do not counsel you to despair. Few things are impossible to diligence and skill. Great works are performed not by strength, but perseverance.
—**SAMUEL JOHNSON**

What this power is I cannot say; all I know is that it exists and it becomes available only when a man is in that state of mind in which he knows exactly what he wants and is fully determined not to quit until he finds it.
—**ALEXANDER GRAHAM BELL**

Tough times never last, but tough people do.
—**ROBERT H. SCHULLER**

Obstacles don't have to stop you. If you run into a wall,
don't turn around and give up. Figure out how to climb it,
go through it, or work around it.
—MICHAEL JORDAN

●

What lies behind you and what lies in front of you
pales in comparison to what lies inside of you.
—RALPH WALDO EMERSON

●

Where the willingness is great, the difficulties cannot be great.
—NICCOLÒ MACHIAVELLI

●

Anyone can hide. Facing up to things, working through them,
that's what makes you strong.
—SARAH DESSEN

●

Life is 10 percent what happens to me and 90 percent of how I react to it.
—CHARLES SWINDOLL

Success is not final, failure is not fatal:

it is the courage to continue that counts.

—SIR WINSTON CHURCHILL

•

Seeds of faith are always within us; sometimes it takes a crisis

to nourish and encourage their growth.

—SUSAN TAYLOR

•

He that cannot endure the bad will not live to see the good.

—YIDDISH PROVERB

•

Every strike brings me closer to the next home run.

—BABE RUTH

•

What this power is I cannot say; all I know is that it exists and

it becomes available only when a man is in that state of mind

in which he knows exactly what he wants and is

fully determined not to quit until he finds it.

—ALEXANDER GRAHAM BELL

Nothing can resist the human will that will stake even
its existence on its stated purpose.
—BENJAMIN DISRAELI

●

There is one kind of robber whom the law does not strike at,
and who steals what is most precious to men: time.
—NAPOLÉON BONAPARTE

●

The longer I live, the more I am certain that the great difference
between the great and the insignificant, its energy—invincible
determination—a purpose once fixed, and then death or victory.
—SIR THOMAS FOWELL BUXTON

●

You can do what you have to do, and sometimes you can
do it even better than you think you can.
—JIMMY CARTER

●

We will either find a way, or make one!
—HANNIBAL

A determined soul will do more with a rusty monkey wrench than a loafer will accomplish with all the tools in a machine shop.
—ROBERT HUGHES

Every worthwhile accomplishment, big or little, has its stages of drudgery and triumph; a beginning, a struggle, and a victory.
—MOHANDAS GANDHI

Bear in mind, if you are going to amount to anything, that your success does not depend upon the brilliancy and the impetuosity with which you take hold, but upon the everlasting and sanctified bulldoggedness with which you hang on after you have taken hold.
—DR. A. B. MELDRUM

A failure establishes only this, that our determination to succeed was not strong enough.
—JOHN CHRISTIAN BOVEE

The price of success is hard work, dedication to the job at hand, and
the determination that whether we win or lose,
we have applied the best of ourselves to the task at hand.
—VINCE LOMBARDI

Patience and perseverance have a magical effect before which
difficulties disappear and obstacles vanish.
—JOHN QUINCY ADAMS

The only good luck many great men ever had was being born with
the ability and determination to overcome bad luck.
—CHANNING POLLOCK

When nothing seems to help, I go and look at a stonecutter
hammering away at his rock perhaps a hundred times without
as much as a crack showing in it. Yet at the hundred and
first blow it will split in two, and I know it was not that blow
that did it—but all that had gone before.
—JACOB RIIS

I am not discouraged, because every wrong attempt discarded

is another step forward.

—THOMAS ALVA EDISON

Ever tried. Ever failed. No matter. Try Again. Fail again. Fail better.

—SAMUEL BECKETT

It's a very funny thing about life; if you refuse to accept

anything but the best, you very often get it.

—W. SOMERSET MAUGHAM

You are the handicap you must face.

You are the one who must choose your place.

—JAMES LANE ALLEN

There are no gains without pains.

—ADLAI STEVENSON

To win without risk is to triumph without glory.

—CORNEILLE

They will rise highest who strive for the highest place.

—LATIN PROVERB

A resolute determination is the truest wisdom.

—NAPOLÉON BONAPARTE

It was courage, faith, endurance, and a dogged determination to
surmount all obstacles that built this bridge.

—JOHN J. WATSON

I learned about the strength you can get from a close family life.
I learned to keep going, even in bad times. I learned not to despair,
even when my world was falling apart. I learned that there are
no free lunches. And I learned the value of hard work.

—LEE IACOCCA

A leader, once convinced that a particular course of action is the
right one, must . . . be undaunted when the going gets tough.
—RONALD REAGAN

•

Fight one more round. When your arms are so tired that you can
hardly lift your hands to come on guard, fight one more round. When
your nose is bleeding and your eyes are black and you are so tired that
you wish your opponent would crack you one on the jaw and put you
to sleep, fight one more round, remembering that the man who always
fights one more round is never whipped.
—JAMES CORBETT

•

If you live long enough, you'll make mistakes. But if you learn from
them, you'll be a better person. It's how you handle adversity, not how
it affects you. The main thing is never quit, never quit, never quit.
—BILL CLINTON

•

The only thing that overcomes hard luck is hard work.
—HARRY GOLDEN

We acquire the strength we have overcome.
—RALPH WALDO EMERSON

You can't run away from trouble. There ain't no place that far.
—JOEL CHANDLER HARRIS

Don't let a bad day make you feel like you have a bad life.
—SOURCE UNKNOWN

Enduring habits I hate. . . . Yes, at the very bottom of my soul I feel grateful to all my misery and bouts of sickness and everything about me that is imperfect, because this sort of thing leaves me with a hundred back doors through which I can escape from enduring habits.
—FRIEDRICH NIETZSCHE

If I had a formula for bypassing trouble, I would not pass it round. Trouble creates a capacity to handle it. I don't embrace trouble; that's as bad as treating it as an enemy. But I do say meet it as a friend, for you'll see a lot of it and had better be on speaking terms with it.
—OLIVER WENDELL HOLMES

Some of God's greatest gifts are unanswered prayers.
—**GARTH BROOKS**

Who will tell whether one happy moment of love or the joy of
breathing or walking on a bright morning and smelling the fresh air, is
not worth all the suffering and effort which life implies.
—**ERICH FROMM**

I ask not for a lighter burden, but for broader shoulders.
—**YIDDISH PROVERB**

You don't know what you can miss before you try.
—**FRANKLIN PIERCE**

I am a slow walker, but I never walk backwards.
—**ABRAHAM LINCOLN**

You may not control all the events that happen to you,
but you can decide not to be reduced by them.
—MAYA ANGELOU

Don't wish it was easier, wish you were better. Don't wish for
less problems, wish for more skills. Don't wish for less challenges,
wish for more wisdom. The major value in life is not what you get.
The major value in life is what you become. Success is not to be
pursued; it is to be attracted by the person you become.
—JIM ROHN

Turn your wounds into wisdom.
—OPRAH WINFREY

We must embrace pain and burn it as fuel for our journey.
—KENJI MIYAZAWA

Adversity is like a strong wind. It tears away from us all but the things
that cannot be torn, so that we see ourselves as we really are.
—ARTHUR GOLDEN

It's not the size of the dog in the fight that counts,

it's the size of the fight in the dog.

—AMERICAN PROVERB

You may not realize it when it happens, but a kick in the teeth may be

the best thing in the world for you.

—WALT DISNEY

The problem is not that there are problems. The problem is expecting

otherwise and thinking that having problems is a problem.

—THEODORE RUBIN

I believe there are more urgent and honorable occupations than the

incomparable waste of time we call suffering.

—SIDONIE-GABRIELLE COLETTE

It takes courage to push yourself to places that you have never been before, to test your limits, to break through barriers. And the day came when the risk it took to remain tight inside the bud was more painful than the risk it took to blossom.

—ANAÏS NIN

•

Watch a man in times of . . . adversity to discover what kind of man he is; for then at last words of truth are drawn from the depths of his heart, and the mask is torn off.

—LUCRETIUS

•

Adversity has the same effect on a man that severe training has on the pugilist: it reduces him to his fighting weight.

—JOSH BILLINGS

•

Smooth seas do not make skillful sailors.

—AFRICAN PROVERB

•

There is no education like adversity.

—BENJAMIN DISRAELI

There are some defeats more triumphant than victories.

—MICHEL DE MONTAIGNE

Adversity introduces a man to himself.

—SOURCE UNKNOWN

In the depths of winter, I finally learned that within me
there lay an invincible summer.

—ALBERT CAMUS

Even our misfortunes are a part of our belongings.

—ANTOINE DE SAINT-EXUPÉRY

If you know someone who tries to drown their sorrows,
you might tell them sorrows know how to swim.

—SOURCE UNKNOWN

It is a common experience that a problem difficult at night is resolved

in the morning after the committee of sleep has worked on it.

—JOHN STEINBECK

Defeat may serve as well as victory to shake the soul and

let the glory out.

—EDWIN MARKHAM

Life didn't promise to be wonderful.

—TEDDY PENDERGRASS

Adversity is the first path to truth.

—LORD BYRON

Every problem has in it the seeds of its own solution.

If you don't have any problems, you don't get any seeds.

—NORMAN VINCENT PEALE

The difficulties of life are intended to make us better, not bitter.
—SOURCE UNKNOWN

A problem is a chance for you to do your best.
—DUKE ELLINGTON

Use your enemy's arrows for firewood.
—MATSHONA DHLIWAYO

They say a reasonable amount o' fleas is good fer a dog—
keeps him from broodin' over bein' a dog, mebbe.
—EDWARD WESTCOTT

Against criticism a man can neither protest nor defend himself;
he must act in spite of it, and then it will gradually yield to him.
—JOHANN WOLFGANG VON GOETHE

Lift up your hearts

Each new hour holds new chances

For new beginnings.

—MAYA ANGELOU

I owe much to my friends; but, all things considered, it strikes me that

I owe even more to my enemies. The real person springs life under a

sting even better than under a caress.

—ANDRÉ GIDE

Although the world is full of suffering,

it is full also of the overcoming of it.

—HELEN KELLER

An arrow can only be shot by pulling it backward. When life is

dragging you back with difficulties, it means it's going to launch you

into something great. So just focus, and keep aiming.

—SOURCE UNKNOWN

Mishaps are like knives that either serve us or cut us,

as we grasp them by the blade or the handle.

—JAMES RUSSELL LOWELL

•

Obstacles are maps inside out.

Troubles are opportunities inside out.

Failures are lessons inside out.

Burdens are blessings inside out.

—MATSHONA DHLIWAYO

•

Problems are only opportunities with thorns on them.

—HUGH MILLER

•

Every flower must grow through dirt.

—SOURCE UNKNOWN

•

There is in every true woman's heart a spark of heavenly fire, which

lies dormant in the broad daylight of prosperity; but which kindles up,

and beams and blazes in the dark hour of adversity.

—WASHINGTON IRVING

The keenest sorrow is to recognize ourselves

as the sole cause of all our adversities.

— **SOPHOCLES**

Have the courage to face a difficulty lest it kick you harder

than you bargained for.

— **STANISLAUS I**

Sometimes I think my life would make a great TV movie. It even has

the part where they say, "Stand by. We are experiencing temporary

difficulties."

— **ROBERT BRAULT**

Perhaps all the dragons of our lives are princesses who are

only waiting to see us once beautiful and brave.

— **RAINER MARIA RILKE**

To have become a deeper man is the privilege of those who have suffered.

— **OSCAR WILDE**

Life is thickly sown with thorns, and I know no other remedy than to pass quickly through them. The longer we dwell on our misfortunes, the greater is their power to harm us.

—VOLTAIRE

The art of living lies less in eliminating our troubles than in growing with them.

—BERNARD M. BARUCH

When life gives you a hundred reasons to cry, show life that you have a thousand reasons to smile.

—SOURCE UNKNOWN

The turning point in the process of growing up is when you discover the core of strength within you that survives all hurt.

—MAX LERNER

Troubles are often the tools by which God fashions us for better things.

—HENRY WARD BEECHER

Don't allow your wounds to turn you into a person you are not.
—SOURCE UNKNOWN

●

Look evil in the face; walk up to it, and you will find it
less than you imagined, and often you will not find it at all;
for it will recede as you advance.
—SYDNEY SMITH

●

Prosperity is a great teacher; adversity is a greater.
—WILLIAM HAZLITT

●

If you want a place in the sun, you've got to expect a few blisters.
—ABIGAIL VAN BUREN

●

The great doctors all got their education off dirt pavements and
poverty—not marble floors and foundations.
—MARTIN H. FISCHER

You'll never find a better sparring partner than adversity.
— **WALT SCHMIDT**

•

Perhaps everything terrible is in its deepest being something

helpless that wants help from us.
— **RAINER MARIA RILKE**

•

If we will be quiet and ready enough,

we shall find compensation in every disappointment.
— **HENRY DAVID THOREAU**

•

The gem cannot be polished without friction nor man without trials.
— **CONFUCIUS**

•

But ne'er the rose without the thorn.
— **ROBERT HERRICK**

Convert difficulties into opportunities, for difficulties
are divine surgeries to make you better.
—SOURCE UNKNOWN

God gave burdens, also shoulders.
—YIDDISH PROVERB

There is something beautiful about all scars of whatever nature. A scar
means the hurt is over, the wound is closed and healed, done with.
—HARRY CREWS

When suffering comes, we yearn for some sign from God,
forgetting we have just had one.
—MIGNON MCLAUGHLIN

Man performs and engenders so much more than he can or should
have to bear. That's how he finds that he can bear anything.
—WILLIAM FAULKNER

The brook would lose its song if you removed the rocks.
—SOURCE UNKNOWN

•

We shall draw from the heart of suffering itself

the means of inspiration and survival.
—SIR WINSTON CHURCHILL

•

Happy is the man who can endure the highest and lowest fortune.

He who has endured such vicissitudes with equanimity

has deprived misfortune of its power.
—SENECA

•

Problems are the price you pay for progress.
—BRANCH RICKEY

•

Scars tell us more about the future than the past, about how we

can live strong despite any pain we've been through.
—TERRI GUILLEMETS

If all misfortunes were laid in one common heap whence
everyone must take an equal portion, most people
would be contented to take their own and depart.
—SOCRATES

There's nothing that cleanses your soul
like getting the hell kicked out of you.
—WOODY HAYES

If you have no confidence in self, you are twice defeated in the race of life.
With confidence, you have won even before you have started.
—MARCUS TULLIUS CICERO

I have heard there are troubles of more than one kind.
Some come from ahead and some come from behind.
But I've bought a big bat. I'm all ready you see.
Now my troubles are going to have troubles with me!
—DR. SEUSS (THEODORE GEISEL)

The misfortunes of mankind are of varied plumage.
—AESCHYLUS

I don't like people who have never fallen or stumbled.

Their virtue is lifeless and it isn't of much value.

Life hasn't revealed its beauty to them.
—BORIS PASTERNAK

We must try not to sink beneath our anguish . . . but battle on.
— J. K. ROWLING

Know yourself and you will win all battles.
—LAO TZU

We look before and after,

And pine for what is not;

Our sincerest laughter

With some pain is fraught;

Our sweetest songs are those that tell of saddest thought.
—PERCY BYSSHE SHELLEY

Count the garden by the flowers, never by the leaves that fall.

Count your life with smiles and not the tears that roll.

— SOURCE UNKNOWN

God brings men into deep waters, not to drown them,

but to cleanse them.

— JOHN AUGHEY

Let me embrace thee, sour adversity,

for wise men say it is the wisest course.

— WILLIAM SHAKESPEARE

Comfort and prosperity have never enriched the world

as much as adversity has.

— BILLY GRAHAM

If you are pained by external things, it is not they that disturb you,

but your own judgment of them. And it is in your power

to wipe out that judgment now.

— MARCUS AURELIUS

Nothing is predestined: The obstacles of your past can
become the gateways that lead to new beginnings.
—RALPH BLUM

The man of virtue makes the difficulty to be overcome his first
business, and success only a subsequent consideration.
—CONFUCIUS

When it gets dark enough, you can see the stars.
—LEE SALK

In spite of rock and tempest's roar,
In spite of false lights on the shore,
Sail on, nor fear to breast the sea!
—HENRY WADSWORTH LONGFELLOW

That which we are, we are;

One equal temper of heroic hearts,

Made weak by time and fate, but strong in will,

To strive, to seek, to find, and not to yield.

—ALFRED, LORD TENNYSON

When I see a man who, bravely,

Meets realities in life,

Who carries on, courageously,

In the face of grief and strife;

Then, I bow my head in honour

Of this man, with courage rare,

Who has such strength of character,

Who, bravely, his burdens bears!

—GERTRUDE T. BUCKINGHAM

In the fell clutch of circumstance
I have not winced nor cried aloud.
Under the bludgeonings of chance
My head is bloody, but unbowed . . .

It matters not how strait the gate,
How charged with punishments the scroll.
I am the master of my fate:
I am the captain of my soul.
—WILLIAM EARNEST HENLEY

Chapter

. . . .

V

On Friendship

Friendship is a deep oneness that develops when two people, speaking the truth in love to one another, journey together to the same horizon.
—TIMOTHY KELLER

The greatest healing therapy is friendship and love.
—HUBERT H. HUMPHREY

If a man does not make new acquaintances as he advances through life, he will soon find himself left alone.
A man, sir, should keep his friendship in a constant repair.
—SAMUEL JOHNSON

The only way to have a friend is to be one.
—RALPH WALDO EMERSON

You'll be richer in the end than a prince, if you're a friend.
—EDGAR A. GUEST

Greater love hath no man than this,

that a man lay down his life for his friends.

—JOHN 15:13

•

The question was once put to [Aristotle], how we ought to

behave to our friends; and the answer he gave was,

As we should wish our friends to behave to us.

—DIOGENES LAERTIUS

•

A friendship that like love is warm;

A love like friendship, steady.

—THOMAS MOORE

•

It takes a year to make a friend, but you can lose one in an hour.

—CHINESE PROVERB

•

Love is the only force capable of transforming an enemy into friend.

—MARTIN LUTHER KING JR.

Friendship! mysterious cement of the soul!

Sweetener of life! and solder of society!

—ROBERT BLAIR

Those friends thou hast, and their adoption tried,

Grapple them to thy soul with hoops of steel.

—WILLIAM SHAKESPEARE

Friendship is one of the sweetest joys of life. Many might have failed

beneath the bitterness of their trial had they not found a friend.

—CHARLES HADDON SPURGEON

One of the most beautiful qualities of true friendship

is to understand and to be understood.

—SENECA

Friendship is as God,

Who gives and asks no payment.

—RICHARD HOVEY

Friendship is Love without his wings.
—**LORD BYRON**

Never tell your friends, I told you so—even when you did.
—**WENDY JEAN SMITH**

Walking with a friend in the dark is better than
walking alone in the light.
—**HELEN KELLER**

Friendship is a sheltering tree.
—**SAMUEL TAYLOR COLERIDGE**

The endearing elegance of female friendship.
—**SAMUEL JOHNSON**

Forsake not an old friend, for the new is not comparable unto him. A new
friend is as new wine: when it is old thou shalt drink it with pleasure.
—**ECCLESIASTES 9:10**

A friend may well be reckoned the masterpiece of Nature.
—**RALPH WALDO EMERSON**

Neither make thy friend equal to a brother; but if thou shalt have made him so, be not the first to do him wrong.
—**HESIOD**

Let the falling out of friends be a renewing of affection.
—**JOHN LYLY**

Distance sometimes endears friendship, and absence sweeteneth it.
—**JAMES HOWELL**

When Zeno was asked what a friend was, he replied, Another I.
—**DIOGENES LAERTIUS**

Old friends are best. King James used to call for his old shoes; they were easiest for his feet.
—**JOHN SELDEN**

Faithful are the wounds of a friend.

—PROVERBS 27:6

Prosperity makes friends, adversity tries them.

—PUBLIUS SYRUS

He used to say that it was better to have one friend of great value
than many friends who were good for nothing.

—DIOGENES LAERTIUS

Honest men esteem and value nothing so much in this world as a real
friend. Such a one is as it were another self, to whom we impart our
most secret thoughts, who partakes of our joy, and comforts us in our
affliction; add to this, that his company is an everlasting pleasure to us.

—BIDPAI

It is a true saying that a man must eat a peck of salt with
his friend before he knows him.

—MIGUEL DE CERVANTES

If instead of a gem, or even a flower, we should cast the gift

of a loving thought into the heart of a friend,

that would be giving as the angels give.

—GEORGE MACDONALD

If you really want to make a friend, go to someone's house and eat with

him. . . . the people who give you their food give you their heart.

—CESAR CHAVEZ

Friendship is the golden thread that ties the heart of all the world.

—JOHN EVELYN

We cannot tell the precise moment when friendship is formed.

As in filling a vessel drop by drop, there is at last a drop

which makes it run over; so in a series of kindnesses

there is at last one which makes the heart run over.

—SAMUEL JOHNSON

A true friend is the greatest of all blessings.

—FRANÇOIS DE LA ROCHEFOUCAULD

True friendship comes when silence between two people is comfortable.

—**DAVE TYSON GENTRY**

The best mirror is an old friend.

—**GEORGE HERBERT**

In order to make friends you must first be friendly.

—**DALE CARNEGIE**

Have no friends not equal to yourself.

—**CONFUCIUS**

It is one of the severest tests of friendship to tell your friend his faults. So to love a man that you cannot bear to see a stain upon him, and to speak painful truth through loving words, that is friendship.

—**HENRY WARD BEECHER**

A friend is a person with whom I may be sincere. Before him I may
think aloud.
—RALPH WALDO EMERSON

Who finds a faithful friend, finds a treasure.
—YIDDISH PROVERB

Friendship is the hardest thing in the world to explain.
It's not something you learn in school. But if you haven't learned the
meaning of friendship, you really haven't learned anything.
—MUHAMMAD ALI

Friendship is the inexpressible comfort of feeling safe with a person,
having neither to weigh thoughts nor measure words.
—GEORGE ELIOT

Friendship is the only cement that will ever hold the world together.
—WOODROW WILSON

Friendship doubles our joy and divides our grief.
—SWEDISH PROVERB

Plant a seed of friendship; reap a bouquet of happiness.
—LOIS L. KAUFMAN

Friendship . . . is born at the moment when one man says to another,
"What! You too? I thought that no one but myself . . ."
—C. S. LEWIS

Don't walk in front of me . . . I may not follow
Don't walk behind me . . . I may not lead
Walk beside me . . . just be my friend.
—ALBERT CAMUS

A friend is someone who knows all about you and still loves you.
—ELBERT HUBBARD

A man that hath friends must show himself friendly; and

there is a friend that sticketh closer than a brother.

—PROVERBS 18:24

•

Good friends, good books, and a sleepy conscience: this is the ideal life.

—MARK TWAIN

•

The truth is, everyone is going to hurt you.

You just got to find the ones worth suffering for.

—BOB MARLEY

•

There is nothing I would not do for those who are really my friends.

I have no notion of loving people by halves, it is not my nature.

—JANE AUSTEN

When we honestly ask ourselves which person in our lives means the most to us, we often find that it is those who, instead of giving advice, solutions, or cures, have chosen rather to share our pain and touch our wounds with a warm and tender hand. The friend who can be silent with us in a moment of despair or confusion, who can stay with us in an hour of grief and bereavement, who can tolerate not knowing, not curing, not healing and face with us the reality of our powerlessness, that is a friend who cares.

—**HENRI J. M. NOUWEN**

The proper office of a friend is to side with you when you are in the wrong. Nearly anybody will side with you when you are in the right.

—**MARK TWAIN**

If you want to know someone's character, look at the friends he keeps.

—**CHINESE PROVERB**

A faithful friend is the medicine of life.

—**APOCRYPHA**

You can't stay in your corner of the Forest waiting for others to come to you. You have to go to them sometimes.
—**A. A. MILNE**

"Why did you do all this for me?" he asked. "I don't deserve it. I've never done anything for you." "You have been my friend," replied Charlotte. "That in itself is a tremendous thing."
—**E. B. WHITE**

I think if I've learned anything about friendship, it's to hang in, stay connected, fight for them, and let them fight for you. Don't walk away, don't be distracted, don't be too busy or tired, don't take them for granted. Friends are part of the glue that holds life and faith together. Powerful stuff.
—**JON KATZ**

To attract good fortune, spend a new coin on an old friend, share an old pleasure with a new friend, and lift up the heart of a true friend by writing his name on the wings of a dragon.
—**CHINESE PROVERB**

How much good inside a day? Depends how good you live 'em.

How much love inside a friend? Depends how much you give 'em.

—SHEL SILVERSTEIN

He must have known I'd want to leave you.

No, he must have known you would always want to come back.

—J. K. ROWLING

No person is your friend who demands your silence,

or denies your right to grow.

—ALICE WALKER

Each friend represents a world in us, a world possibly not born until

they arrive, and it is only by this meeting that a new world is born.

—ANAÏS NIN

Do I not destroy my enemies when I make them my friends?

—ABRAHAM LINCOLN

Why is it, he said, one time, at the subway entrance,

I feel I've known you so many years?

Because I like you, she said, and I don't want anything from you.

—RAY BRADBURY

If you have two friends in your lifetime, you're lucky.

If you have one good friend, you're more than lucky.

—S. E. HINTON

Words are easy, like the wind; Faithful friends are hard to find.

—WILLIAM SHAKESPEARE

Growing apart doesn't change the fact that for a long time we grew

side by side; our roots will always be tangled. I'm glad for that.

—ALLY CONDIE

The sweetest grapes are picked from the vineyard of friendship.

—FRENCH PROVERB

Silences make the real conversations between friends.

Not the saying, but the never needing to say that counts.

—**MARGARET LEE RUNBECK**

The worst part of success is trying to find someone who is happy for you.

—**BETTE MIDLER**

Tis the privilege of friendship to talk nonsense,

and to have her nonsense respected.

—**CHARLES LAMB**

May the hinges of our friendship never grow rusty.

—**IRISH BLESSING**

The capacity for friendship is God's way of apologizing for our families.

—**JAY MCINERNEY**

Friendship is an empty word if it only works one way.

—**ALBANIAN PROVERB**

The glory of friendship is not the outstretched hand,
not the kindly smile, nor the joy of companionship; it is the spiritual
inspiration that comes to one when you discover that someone else
believes in you and is willing to trust you with a friendship.
—RALPH WALDO EMERSON

•

Friendship marks a life even more deeply than love. Love risks
degenerating into obsession, friendship is never anything but sharing.
—ELIE WIESEL

•

Friendship—my definition—is built on two things. Respect and trust.
Both elements have to be there. And it has to be mutual.
You can have respect for someone, but if you don't have trust,
the friendship will crumble.
—STIEG LARSSON

•

Never leave a friend behind. Friends are all we have to
get us through this life—and they are the only things
from this world that we could hope to see in the next.
—DEAN KOONTZ

When I say it's you I like, I'm talking about that part of you that knows that life is far more than anything you can ever see or hear or touch. That deep part of you that allows you to stand for those things without which humankind cannot survive. Love that conquers hate, peace that rises triumphant over war, and justice that proves more powerful than greed.

—FRED ROGERS

"Stay" is a charming word in a friend's vocabulary.

—AMOS BRONSON ALCOTT

You can go through life and make new friends every year—every month practically—but there was never any substitute for those friendships of childhood that survive into adult years. Those are the ones in which we are bound to one another with hoops of steel.

—ALEXANDER MCCALL SMITH

Friendship is the bestiest thing that comes to life.

—MARILYN MONROE

A man should choose a friend who is better than himself.
—**CHINESE PROVERB**

The friend who holds your hand and says the wrong thing is made of
dearer stuff than the one who stays away.
—**BARBARA KINGSOLVER**

Sometimes being a friend means mastering the art of timing.
There is a time for silence. A time to let go and allow people to hurl
themselves into their own destiny. And a time to prepare
to pick up the pieces when it's all over.
—**GLORIA NAYLOR**

Friendship is a plant we must often water.
—**GERMAN PROVERB**

Wishing to be friends is quick work,

but friendship is a slow ripening fruit.

—**ARISTOTLE**

•

May your friendship not be like a stone: if it breaks you cannot

put the pieces together. May it be like iron: when it breaks,

you can weld the pieces back together.

—**MALAGASY BLESSING**

Chapter

VI

On Love

Love conquers all things, so we too shall yield to love.
—VIRGIL

Any time not spent on love is wasted.
—TORQUATO TASSO

If I had a flower for every time I thought of you . . .
I could walk through my garden forever.
—ALFRED, LORD TENNYSON

A kiss on the beach when there is a full moon
is the closest thing to heaven.
—H. JACKSON BROWN JR.

To love another person is to see the face of God.
—VICTOR HUGO

Love is patient and kind, Love is not jealous, conceited, proud,
or boastful, it is not arrogant, selfish, irritable, or rude.
Love does not keep a record of wrongs. Love is not happy with evil,
but is happy with the truth, Love never gives up, and
its faith, hope, and patience never fail. Love is eternal.
—1 CORINTHIANS 13

Age does not protect you from love.
But love, to some extent, protects you from age.
—ANAÏS NIN

To get the full value of joy, you must have someone to divide it with.
—MARK TWAIN

To be loved, be loveable.
—OVID

Those who love deeply never grow old;
they may die of old age, but they die young.
—DOROTHY CANFIELD FISHER

The greatest happiness of life is the conviction that we are loved—
loved for ourselves, or rather, loved in spite of ourselves.
—VICTOR HUGO

Love is the flower of life, and blossoms unexpectedly and
without law, and must be plucked where it is found, and
enjoyed for the brief hour of its duration.
—D. H. LAWRENCE

I love you as certain dark things are to be loved,
in secret, between the shadow and the soul.
—PABLO NERUDA

Every heart sings a song, incomplete, until another heart
whispers back. Those who wish to sing always find a song.
At the touch of a lover, everyone becomes a poet.
—PLATO

Love doesn't make the world go round.

Love is what makes the ride worthwhile.

—FRANKLIN P. JONES

Where there is love, there is life.

—MOHANDAS GANDHI

The first to apologize is the bravest. The first to forgive is the strongest. The first to forget is the happiest.

—SOURCE UNKNOWN

And in the end, the love you take is equal to the love you make.

—JOHN LENNON AND PAUL MCCARTNEY

Love is always bestowed as a gift—freely, willingly, and without expectation. We don't love to be loved, we love to love.

—LEO BUSCAGLIA

Love is an act of endless forgiveness,
a tender look which becomes a habit.
—PETER USTINOV

•

Love is the master key that opens the gates of happiness.
—OLIVER WENDELL HOLMES

•

There is no greater happiness for a man than approaching a door
at the end of a day knowing someone on the other side of
that door is waiting for the sound of his footsteps.
—RONALD REAGAN

•

Love is the condition in which the happiness of
another person is essential to your own.
—ROBERT HEINLEIN

•

I got gaps; you got gaps; we fill each other's gaps.
—SYLVESTER STALLONE (AS ROCKY BALBOA)

Love is like a friendship caught on fire. In the beginning a flame,
very pretty, often hot and fierce, but still only light and flickering.
As love grows older, our hearts mature and our love becomes as coals,
deep-burning and unquenchable.
—JOSEPH ADDISON

The best love is the one that makes you a better person, without
changing you into someone other than yourself.
—SOURCE UNKNOWN

We waste time looking for the perfect lover,
instead of creating the perfect love.
—TOM ROBBINS

New love is the brightest and long love is the greatest.
But revived love is the tenderest thing known on earth.
—THOMAS HARDY

Life is slippery. We all need a loving hand to hold onto.
—H. JACKSON BROWN JR.

Love is just a word until someone comes along and gives it meaning.

—SOURCE UNKNOWN

There is only one happiness in life; to love and be loved.

—GEORGE SAND

It is love, not reason, that is stronger than death.

—THOMAS MANN

The heart has its reasons which reason knows nothing of.

—BLAISE PASCAL

Love can turn a cottage into a golden palace.

—GERMAN PROVERB

Don't compare your love story to those you watch in movies.

They're written by screenwriters, yours is written by God.

—SOURCE UNKNOWN

Love is a promise; love is a souvenir, once given never forgotten,

never let it disappear.

— **JOHN LENNON**

Being deeply loved by someone gives you strength,

while loving someone deeply gives you courage.

— **LAO TZU**

Love is life. If you miss love, you miss life.

— **LEO BUSCAGLIA**

We love the things we love for what they are.

— **ROBERT FROST**

Love is like the wind. You can't see it but you can feel it.

— **NICHOLAS SPARKS**

It is love that makes the impossible possible.

— **INDIAN PROVERB**

Of all forms of caution, caution in love is perhaps
the most fatal to true happiness.
—BERTRAND RUSSELL

Love is when you meet someone who tells you
something new about yourself.
—ANDRE BRETON

Where we love is home—home that our feet may leave,
but not our hearts.
—OLIVER WENDELL HOLMES SR.

Absence is to love as wind is to fire;
it extinguishes the small and kindles the great.
—ROGER DE MONTAI-RABUTIN

I have found the paradox, that if you love until it hurts,
there can be no more hurt, only more love.
—MOTHER TERESA

Love puts the fun in together, the sad in apart, and the joy in a heart.
—SOURCE UNKNOWN

The best proof of love is trust.
—DR. JOYCE BROTHERS

Life is the flower for which love is the honey.
—VICTOR HUGO

Keep love in your heart. A life without it is like a sunless garden when the flowers are dead. The consciousness of loving and being loved brings a warmth and richness to life that nothing else can bring.
—OSCAR WILDE

There is no remedy for love but to love more.
—HENRY DAVID THOREAU

True love begins when nothing is looked for in return.
—ANTOINE DE SAINT-EXUPÉRY

This is the miracle that happens every time to those who really love;

the more they give, the more they possess.

—RAINER MARIA RILKE

•

I can't say anymore than I love you.

Anything else would be a waste of breath.

—ELVIS COSTELLO

•

I miss you a little, I guess you could say, a little too much,

a little too often, and a little more each day.

—SOURCE UNKNOWN

•

Love sees roses without thorns.

—GERMAN PROVERB

•

Love does not consist in gazing at each other,

but in looking outward in the same direction.

—ANTOINE DE SAINT-EXUPÉRY

You know you're in love when you can't fall asleep because
reality is finally better than your dreams.
—DR. SEUSS (THEODORE GEISEL)

No relationship is all sunshine, but once you've learned
how to play in the rain, you've discovered the secret to
surviving the passing storm together.
—SOURCE UNKNOWN

Whatever our souls are made of, his and mine are the same.
—EMILY BRONTË

Love seems the swiftest but it is the slowest of all growths.
No man or woman really knows what perfect love is
until they have been married a quarter of a century.
—MARK TWAIN

No road is long with good company.
—TURKISH PROVERB

Love is no assignment for cowards.

—OVID

The best love is the kind that awakens the soul and
makes us reach for more, that plants a fire in our hearts
and brings peace to our minds.

—NICHOLAS SPARKS

Sexiness wears thin after a while, and beauty fades.
But to be married to a man who makes you laugh every day,
ah, now that's a real treat.

—JOANNE WOODWARD

Being deeply loved by someone gives you strength while
loving someone deeply gives you courage.

—LAO TZU

The first duty of love is to listen.

—PAUL TILLICH

Our partner is essential to the discovery of our own calling, and
in a curious way shows us what we want, or more exactly, shows us
what is wanted of us from within ourselves and our world.

—THOMAS MOORE

Love is what you've been through with somebody.

—JAMES THURBER

Two persons who love each other are in a place
more holy than the interior of a church.

—WILLIAM LYON PHELPS

Let us no more contend, nor blame each other,
blamed enough elsewhere, but strive, In offices of love,
how we may lighten each other's burden.

—JOHN MILTON

Where there's marriage without love,
there will be love without marriage.

—BENJAMIN FRANKLIN

A wise physician once said, "The best medicine for humans is love."

Someone asked, "What if it doesn't work?"

He smiled and answered, "Increase the dose."

—SOURCE UNKNOWN

I chose my wife as she did her wedding-gown, not for a fine glossy surface, but for such qualities as would wear well.

—OLIVER GOLDSMITH

Before marriage, a man will lie awake thinking about something you said; after marriage he'll fall asleep before you finish saying it.

—HELEN ROWLAND

By all means marry; if you get a good wife, you'll become happy; if you get a bad one, you'll become a philosopher.

—SOCRATES

The heart that loves is always young.

—GREEK PROVERB

She who dwells with me whom I have loved with such communion,
that no place on earth can ever be solitude to me.
—WILLIAM BLAKE

Marriage is not the ritual or an end, it is a long, intricate, intimate
dance together and nothing matters more than your own
sense of balance and choice of partner.
—AMY BLOOM

I have lived long enough to know that the evening glow of love
has its own riches and splendour.
—BENJAMIN DISRAELI

All the world loves a lover.
—ENGLISH PROVERB

The goal in marriage is not to think alike, but to think together.
—SOURCE UNKNOWN

What greater thing is there for two human souls than to feel that
they are joined . . . to beat one with each other in silent,
unspeakable memories.
—GEORGE ELIOT

Let there be spaces in your togetherness.
—KAHLIL GIBRAN

The best thing to hold onto in life is . . . each other.
—AUDREY HEPBURN

Where we love, is home. Home that our feet may leave,
but not our hearts.
—OLIVER WENDELL HOLMES

There is no physician who can cure the disease of love.
—AFRICAN PROVERB

When the heart is flooded with love there is no room in it for fear, for doubt, for hesitation. And it is this lack of fear that makes for the dance. When each partner loves so completely that he has forgotten to ask himself whether he is loved in return; when he only knows that he loves and is moving to music—then, and then only, are two people able to dance perfectly in time to the same rhythm.

—ANNE MORROW LINDBERGH

Once the realization is accepted that even between
the closest human beings, infinite distances continue,
a wonderful living, side by side, can grow.

—RAINER MARIA RILKE

When you fish for love, bait with your heart, not your brain.

—MARK TWAIN

Where love sets the table, food tastes at its best.

—FRENCH PROVERB

The most wonderful of all things in life, I believe, is the discovery of another human being with whom one's relationship has a growing depth, beauty and joy as the years increase. This inner progressiveness of love between two human beings is a most marvelous thing, it cannot be found by looking for it, or by passionately wishing for it. It is a sort of divine accident and the most wonderful of all things in life.

—HUGH WALPOLE

A dream you dream alone is only a dream.
A dream you dream together becomes reality.

—JOHN LENNON

There is no substitute for the comfort supplied by the utterly taken-for-granted relationship.

—IRIS MURDOCH

Make sure you never, never argue at night. You just lose a good night's sleep, and you can't settle anything until morning anyway.

—ROSE F. KENNEDY

Love allows your beloved the freedom to be unlike you.

Attachment asks for conformity to your needs and desires . . .

Love expands beyond the limits of two people.

Attachment tries to exclude everything but two people.

—**DEEPAK CHOPRA**

Love does not begin and end the way we seem to think it does.

Love is a battle, love is a war; love is a growing up.

—**JAMES BALDWIN**

One who loves the vase loves also what is inside.

—**AFRICAN PROVERB**

An old man in love is like a flower in winter.

—**CHINESE PROVERB**

I hold it true, whate'er befall;

I feel it, when I sorrow most;

'Tis better to have loved and lost

Than never to have loved at all.

—ALFRED, LORD TENNYSON

Don't smother each other. No one can grow in the shade.

—LEO BUSCAGLIA

Many waters cannot quench love; rivers cannot wash it away.

If one were to give all the wealth of his house for love,

it would be utterly scorned.

—SONG OF SONGS 8:7

Old love does not rust.

—ESTONIAN PROVERB

How do I love thee? Let me count the ways.

I love thee to the depth and breadth and height

My soul can reach, when feeling out of sight

For the ends of Being and ideal Grace.

I love thee to the level of everyday's

Most quiet need, by sun and candle-light.

I love thee freely, as men strive for Right;

I love thee purely, as they turn from Praise.

I love thee with a passion put to use

In my old griefs, and with my childhood's faith.

I love thee with a love I seemed to lose

With my lost saints, —I love thee with the breath,

Smiles, tears, of all my life!

—and, if God choose, I shall but love thee better after death.

—ELIZABETH BARRETT BROWNING

Let me not to the marriage of true minds
Admit impediments. Love is not love
Which alters when it alteration finds,
Or bends with the remover to remove:
O no; it is an ever-fixed mark,
That looks on tempests, and is never shaken;
It is the star to every wandering bark,
Whose worth's unknown, although his height be taken.
Love's not Time's fool, though rosy lips and cheeks
Within his bending sickle's compass come;
Love alters not with his brief hours and weeks,
But bears it out even to the edge of doom.
If this be error and upon me proved,
I never writ, nor no man ever loved.
—**WILLIAM SHAKESPEARE, SONNET 116**

Chapter
· · · · · · · · · · · ·
VII

On Marriage

The sum that two married people owe to one
another defies calculation. It is an infinite debt,
which can only be discharged through eternity.
—JOHANN WOLFGANG VON GOETHE

Married couples who love each other tell each other
a thousand things without talking.
—CHINESE PROVERB

A happy marriage is the union of two good forgivers.
—ROBERT QUILLEN

Love is a flower which turns into fruit at marriage.
—FINNISH PROVERB

The most important thing a father can do for
his children is to love their mother.
—REV. THEODORE HESBURGH

What a happy and holy fashion it is that those who love
one another should rest on the same pillow.
—NATHANIEL HAWTHORNE

A long marriage is two people trying to dance
a duet and two solos at the same time.
—ANNE TAYLOR FLEMING

The more you invest in a marriage, the more valuable it becomes.
—AMY GRANT

To keep your marriage brimming, with love in the wedding cup,
whenever you're wrong, admit it; whenever you're right, shut up.
—OGDEN NASH

The highest happiness on earth is the happiness of marriage.
—WILLIAM LYON PHELPS

Choose your wife as you wish your children to be.
—**GAELIC PROVERB**

•

Many marriages would be better if the husband and wife
clearly understood that they are on the same side.
—**HILARY "ZIG" ZIGLAR**

•

Love is an ideal thing, marriage a real thing.
—**JOHANN WOLFGANG VON GOETHE**

•

People stay married because they want to,
not because the doors are locked.
—**PAUL NEWMAN**

•

Marriage, ultimately, is the practice of becoming passionate friends.
—**HARVILLE HENDRIX**

Once we figured out that we could not change each other,

we became free to celebrate ourselves as we are.

—H. DEAN RUTHERFORD

(IN A LETTER TO HIS WIFE ON THEIR

FIFTY-NINTH WEDDING ANNIVERSARY)

A good marriage is a contest of generosity.

—DIANE SAWYER

Marriage is like a fine wine; if tended properly,

it just gets better with age.

—SOURCE UNKNOWN

Don't marry the person you think you can live with;

marry only the individual you think you can't live without.

—JAMES C. DOBSON

If ever two were one, then surely we.

If ever man were loved by wife, then thee.

If ever wife was happy in a man,

Compare with me, ye women, if you can.

I prize thy love more than whole mines of gold,

Or all the riches that the East doth hold.

My love is such that rivers cannot quench,

Nor ought but love from thee give recompense.

Thy love is such I can no way repay;

The heavens reward thee manifold, I pray.

Then while we live, in love let's so persever,

That when we live no more we may live ever.

—ANNE BRADSTREET

One advantage of marriage is that, when you fall out of love

with him or he falls out of love with you,

it keeps you together until you fall in again.

—JUDITH VIORST

When there is love in a marriage, there is harmony in the home; when
there is harmony in the home, there is contentment in the community;
when there is contentment in the community, there is prosperity
in the nation; when there is prosperity in the nation,
there is peace in the world.
—CHINESE PROVERB

The couple who prays together, stays together.
—SOURCE UNKNOWN

Love at first sight is easy to understand; it's when two people have
been looking at each other for a lifetime that it becomes a miracle.
—SAM LEVINSON

There is no greater risk than matrimony.
But there is nothing happier than a happy marriage.
—BENJAMIN DISRAELI

The most precious gift that marriage gave me was the constant impact
of something very close and intimate, yet all the time
unmistakably other, resistant—in a word, real.
—C. S. LEWIS

•

A good marriage is that in which
each appoints the other guardian of his solitude.
—RAINER MARIA RILKE

•

The secret of a happy marriage is finding the right person. You know
they're right if you love to be with them all of the time.
—JULIA CHILD

•

Only choose in marriage a man whom you would
choose as a friend if he were a woman.
—JOSEPH JOUBERT

Marriage does not guarantee you will be together forever, it's only paper. It takes love, respect, trust, understanding, friendship, and faith in your relationship to make it last.

—SOURCE UNKNOWN

●

A good marriage is one which allows for change and growth in the individuals and in the way they express their love.

—PEARL BUCK

●

Your gift to me is uninsurable. No appraiser can put a value on it. . . . It's like fruit of the month or a lifetime subscription—a perpetual-motion happiness machine. It starts off fresh and brand new every day, shining up my whole world. . . .

—RONALD REAGAN (IN A LETTER TO HIS WIFE, NANCY)

●

A happy marriage has in it all the pleasures of friendship, all the enjoyment of sense and reason—and indeed all the sweets of life.

—JOSEPH ADDISON

Write a list of ways that you have benefited from being married to your spouse. Then write a list of your spouse's positive patterns and qualities. Keep adding to the lists and reread them frequently.

—RABBI ZELIG PLISKIN

There is no more lovely, friendly, and charming relationship, communion, or company than a good marriage.

—MARTIN LUTHER

Marriage is a recognition of a spiritual identity.

—JOSEPH CAMPBELL

To keep the fire burning brightly there's one easy rule: Keep the two logs together, near enough to keep each other warm and far enough apart—about a finger's breadth—for breathing room. Good fire, good marriage, same rule.

—MARNIE REED CROWELL

The bonds of matrimony are like any other bonds—they mature slowly.

—PETER DE VRIES

Oh! Surely marriage is a great and sacred responsibility.
It is a bark in which two souls venture out on life's stormy sea,
with no aid but their own to help them.

—JAMES HAMILTON

A good marriage is one which allows for change and growth in the
individuals and the way they express their love.

—PEARL S. BUCK

The real marriage of true minds is for any two people to possess a sense
of humor or irony pitched in exactly the same key, so that their joint
glances at any subject cross like interarching searchlights.

—EDITH WHARTON

The man who has entered into a beautiful union is sure of at least one
person to whom he can give the best that he possesses.

—GEORGES DUHAMEL

The happy State of Matrimony is, undoubtedly, the surest and
most lasting Foundation of Comfort and Love . . .
the Cause of all good Order in the World, and
what alone preserves it from the utmost Confusion.
— BENJAMIN FRANKLIN

What counts in making a happy marriage is not so much how
compatible you are, but how you deal with incompatibility.
— LEO TOLSTOY

The great secret of successful marriage is to treat all disasters as
incidents and none of the incidents as disasters.
— SIR HAROLD NICOLSON

One of the nicest things you can say to your partner,
"If I had it to do over again, I'd choose you. Again."
— SOURCE UNKNOWN

One of the good things that come of a true marriage is, that there is
one face which changes come without you seeing them; or rather,
there is one face which you can see the same, through
all the shadows which years have gathered upon it.

— GEORGE MACDONALD

A happy marriage is a long conversation that seems all too short.

— ANDRE MAUROIS

Ruth and I are happily incompatible.

— REV. BILLY GRAHAM (WHEN ASKED HIS SECRET OF BEING
MARRIED FIFTY-FOUR YEARS TO THE SAME PERSON)

Chains do not hold a marriage together. It is threads, hundreds of
tiny threads which sew people together through the years.

— SIMONE SIGNORET

Happy is the man who finds a true friend, and far happier is
he who finds that true friend in his wife.

— FRANZ SCHUBERT

It's true what they say—all the good men are married.

But it's marriage that makes them good.

— GAY TALESE

When a wife has a good husband, it is easily seen on her face.

— JOHANN WOLFGANG VON GOETHE

What greater thing is there for two human souls than to feel that
they are joined for life—to strengthen each other in all labor,
to rest on each other in all sorrow, to minister to each other
in all pain, to be one with each other in silent, unspeakable
memories at the moment of the last parting.

— GEORGE ELIOT

A marriage makes of two fractional lives a whole;
it gives to two purposeless lives a work and doubles the
strength of each to perform it. It gives to two questioning
natures a reason for living and something to live for.

— MARK TWAIN

I think a man and a woman should choose each other for life, for the simple reason that a long life with all its accidents is barely enough time for a man and a woman to understand each other and . . .

to understand—is to love.

—WILLIAM BUTLER YEATS

●

A successful marriage is an edifice that must be rebuilt every day.

—ANDRE MAUROIS

●

A life allied with mine, for the rest of our lives . . .

that is the miracle of marriage.

—DENIS DE ROUGEMONT

In a successful marriage, there is no such thing as one's way.
There is only the way of both, only the bumpy, dusty, difficult,
but always mutual path.
—PHYLLIS MCGINLEY

A marriage wish: One year of joy, another of comfort, and
all the rest of content.
—ENGLISH PROVERB

To continue to love in marriage is a science.
—MADAM REYBAUD

Let husband and wife neglect the whole world besides,
rather than one another.
—SOURCE UNKNOWN

Marriage is not, like the hill of Olympus, wholly clear without clouds.
—THOMAS FULLER

Marriage like government is a series of compromises.

One must give and take, repair and restrain, endure and be patient.

—SAMUEL SMILES

Marriage is not just spiritual communion and passionate embraces;

marriage is also three meals a day, sharing the workload, and

remembering to carry out the trash.

—DR. JOYCE BROTHERS

Marriage the happiest bond of love might be,

If hands were only joined when hearts agree.

—GEORGE GRANVILLE

In marriage never taunt with a past mistake.

—SOURCE UNKNOWN

The married should not forget that to speak of love begets love.

—BLAISE PASCAL

A good marriage in it . . . all the pleasures of a friendship,

all the enjoyments of sense and reason, and

indeed all the sweets of life.

—JOSEPH ADDISON

Same old slippers—Same old rice—Same old glimpse of paradise.

—WILLIAM JAMES LAMPTON

One should believe in marriage as in the immortality of the soul.

—HONORÉ DE BALZAC

Chapter

· · · · · · · · · · ·

VIII

On Childhood and Youth

Youth has no age.
—PABLO PICASSO

Blessed be childhood, which brings down something of
heaven into the midst of our rough earthliness.
—HENRI FREDERIC AMIEL

Youth is happy because it has the ability to see beauty.
Anyone who keeps the ability to see beauty never grows old.
—FRANZ KAFKA

A team is where a boy can prove his courage on his own.
A gang is where a coward goes to hide.
—MICKEY MANTLE

I'm youth, I'm joy, I'm a little bird that has broken out of the egg.
—SIR JAMES M. BARRIE

He who takes a child by the hand takes a mother by the heart.
—DANISH PROVERB

You are only young once, and if you work it right, once is enough.
—JOE E. LEWIS

We cannot always build the future for our youth,
but we can build our youth for the future.
—FRANKLIN D. ROOSEVELT

Rejoice, O young man, in thy youth; and let thy heart cheer thee
in the days of thy youth, and walk in the ways of thine heart,
and in the sight of thine eyes: but know thou,
that for all these things God will bring thee into judgment.
—ECCLESIASTES 11:9

A youth that does not cultivate friendship with
the elderly is like a tree without roots.
—NTOMBAN PROVERB

In youth, we clothe ourselves with rainbows,

and go as brave as the zodiac.

—RALPH WALDO EMERSON

Alas, that Spring should vanish with the Rose!

That Youth's sweet-scented Manuscript should close!

—OMAR KHAYYAM

Being young is a fault that improves daily.

—SWEDISH PROVERB

Youth comes but once in a lifetime.

—HENRY WADSWORTH LONGFELLOW

Youth itself is a talent—a perishable talent.

—ERIC HOFFER

Good habits formed at youth make all the difference.

—ARISTOTLE

Age considers; youth ventures.
—**RABINDRANATH TAGORE**

Fame is the thirst of youth.
—**LORD BYRON**

Our youth we can have but to-day,
We may always find time to grow old.
—**GEORGE BERKLEY**

A hundred things are done today in the divine name of Youth,
that if they showed their true colors would be seen
by rights to belong rather to old age.
—**WYNDHAM LEWIS**

The good thing about being young is that you are not experienced
enough to know you cannot possibly do the things you are doing.
—**GENE BROWN**

It is not possible for civilization to flow backwards while
there is youth in the world. Youth may be headstrong,
but it will advance it allotted length.
—HELEN KELLER

•

Children are poor men's riches.
—ENGLISH PROVERB

•

The Youth of a Nation are the trustees of posterity.
—BENJAMIN DISRAELI

•

Youth is the time to go flashing from one end of the world to the other
to try the manners of different nations; to hear the chimes at midnight;
to see the sunrise in town and country; to be converted at a revival; to
circumnavigate the metaphysics, write halting verses, run a mile to see
a fire, and wait all day long in the theatre to applaud *Hernani.*
—ROBERT LOUIS STEVENSON

Use your youth so that you may have comfort to remember it when it has forsaken you, and not sigh and grieve at the account thereof.
—SIR WALTER RALEIGH

•

We've begun to raise daughters more like sons . . . but few have the courage to raise our sons more like our daughters.
—GLORIA STEINEM

•

Your children are not your children/They are the sons and daughters of Life's longing for itself.
—KAHLIL GIBRAN

•

Youth is such a wonderful thing. What a crime to waste it on children.
—GEORGE BERNARD SHAW

They—Young People have exalted notions, because they have not
been humbled by life or learned its necessary limitations; moreover,
their hopeful disposition makes them think themselves equal to great
things—and that means having exalted notions. They would always
rather do noble deeds than useful ones: Their lives are regulated
more by moral feeling than by reasoning—all their mistakes
are in the direction of doing things excessively and vehemently.
They overdo everything—they love too much, hate too much, and the
same with everything else.

—ARISTOTLE

Children are the true connoisseurs.
What's precious to them has no price—only value.

—BEL KAUFMAN

In automotive terms, the child supplies the power
but the parents have to do the steering.

—DR. BENJAMIN SPOCK

Enjoy the Spring of Love and Youth, to some good angel

leave the rest; For Time will teach thee soon the truth,

there are no birds in last year's nest!

—HENRY WADSWORTH LONGFELLOW

Youth is the best time to be rich, and the best time to be poor.

—EURIPIDES

The search after the great men is the dream of youth,

and the most serious occupation of manhood.

—RALPH WALDO EMERSON

Children know the grace of God/Better than most of us.

They see the world the way that morning brings it back

to them/New and born and fresh and wonderful.

—ARCHIBALD MACLEISH

Youth, with swift feet, walks onward in the way;

the land of joy lies all before his eyes.

—EDWARD BULWER-LYTTON

Youth gets together with their materials to build a bridge to the moon
or maybe a palace on earth; then in middle age
they decide to build a woodshed with them instead.
—HENRY DAVID THOREAU

Childhood shows the man, as morning shows the day.
—JOHN MILTON

It is better to be a young June bug than an old bird of paradise.
—MARK TWAIN

A boy's story is the best that is ever told.
—CHARLES DICKENS

I am not young enough to know everything.
—OSCAR WILDE

Life's aspirations come in the guise of children.
—RABINDRANATH TAGORE

No man knows he is young while he is young.

—**G. K. CHESTERTON**

◦

The young man shows what the old man was.

—**SWEDISH PROVERB**

◦

Extend your "best before" date by living a youthful life.

—**LORI MYERS**

◦

Remember that as a teenager you are at the last stage in your life when you will be happy to hear that the phone is for you.

—**FRAN LEBOWITZ**

◦

Every youth owes it to himself and to the world to make the most possible out of the stuff that is in him. . . .

—**ORISON SWETT MARDEN**

◦

A baby is an angel whose wings decrease as his legs increase.

—**FRENCH PROVERB**

At the age of six I wanted to be a cook. At seven I wanted to be Napoléon. And my ambition has been growing steadily ever since.
—SALVADOR DALÍ

Confusion is a luxury which only the very, very young can possibly afford and you are not that young anymore.
—JAMES BALDWIN

Children are God's apostles, day by day/Sent forth to preach of love and hope and peace.
—JAMES RUSSELL LOWELL

When I was a boy of fourteen, my father was so ignorant I could hardly stand to have the old man around. But when I got to be twenty-one, I was astonished at how much the old man had learned in seven years.
—JOSH BILLINGS

I remember my youth and the feeling that will never come back any more—the feeling that I could last for ever, outlast the sea, the earth, and all men; the deceitful feeling that lures us on to joys, to perils, to love, to vain effort—to death; the triumphant conviction of strength, the heat of life in the handful of dust, the glow in the heart that with every year grows dim, grows cold, grows small, and expires—and expires, too soon, too soon—before life itself.

—JOSEPH CONRAD

Youth! There is nothing like youth. The middle-aged are mortgaged to Life. The old are in Life's lumber-room. But youth is the Lord of Life. Youth has a kingdom waiting for it. Every one is born a king, and most people die in exile.

—OSCAR WILDE

The arrogance of age must submit to be taught by youth.

—EDMUND BURKE

Children are the anchors that hold a mother to life.
— SOPHOCLES

•

The deepest definition of youth is life as yet untouched by tragedy.
— ALFRED NORTH WHITEHEAD

•

How beautiful is youth! how bright it gleams with its illusions,
aspirations, dreams! Book of Beginnings, Story without End,
Each maid a heroine, and each man a friend!
— HENRY WADSWORTH LONGFELLOW

•

We find delight in the beauty and happiness of children
that makes the heart too big for the body.
— RALPH WALDO EMERSON

•

Youth is wholly experimental.
— ROBERT LOUIS STEVENSON

Every goose thinks its gosling is a swan.
—DANISH PROVERB

There is nothing can pay one for that invaluable ignorance which is the companion of youth, those sanguine groundless hopes, and that lively vanity which makes all the happiness of life.
—LADY MARY WORTLEY MONTAGU

The young do not know enough to be prudent, and therefore they attempt the impossible—and achieve it, generation after generation.
—PEARL S. BUCK

Give a little love to a child, and you get a great deal back.
—JOHN RUSKIN

What good mothers and fathers instinctively feel like doing for their babies is usually best after all.
—DR. BENJAMIN SPOCK

Young people think they never can change, but they do in the
most wonderful manner, and very few die of broken hearts.
—**LOUISA MAY ALCOTT**

•

We like rather to dream of a body of young men as a live thing, as a
tree where all the branches are nourished by a single sap, and where
each part is meaningless and incomplete except in connection with its
fellows. You may lop away the dead branches, you may bend the trunk,
you may dig about it and water it; but leave it to assume its own form,
do not constrain the peculiar roots, or you will have a crippled,
gnarled monster, and no tree.
—**LEARNED HAND**

Chapter
· · · · · · · · · · ·
IX

On Aging

No wise man ever wished to be younger.

—JONATHAN SWIFT

•

Aging is not lost youth but a new stage of opportunity and strength.

—BETTY FRIEDAN

•

Youth is the gift of nature, but age is a work of art.

—STANISLAW LEC

•

We don't grow older, we grow riper.

—PABLO PICASSO

•

Gray hair is a glorious crown won by a righteous life.

—YIDDISH PROVERB

•

You can be gorgeous at thirty, charming at forty, and
irresistible for the rest of your life.

—COCO CHANEL

The older the fiddle, the sweeter the tune.

—AMERICAN PROVERB

•

I live in that solitude which is painful in youth,

but delicious in the years of maturity.

—ALBERT EINSTEIN

•

Age is something that doesn't matter, unless you are a cheese.

—BILLIE BURKE

•

"Age" is the acceptance of a term of years.

But maturity is the glory of years.

—MARTHA GRAHAM

•

As we grow old, the beauty steals inward.

—RALPH WALDO EMERSON

The denunciation of the young is a necessary part of the hygiene of
older people, and greatly assists the circulation of their blood.
—LOGAN PEARSALL SMITH

Human beings are pampered by the Lord.
Their real tests don't come until later in life.
—WILLIE STARGELL

Youth, large, lusty, loving—Youth, full of grace, force, fascination!
Do you know that Old Age may come after you,
with equal grace, force, fascination?
—WALT WHITMAN

Youth, which is forgiven everything, forgives itself nothing:
age, which forgives itself everything, is forgiven nothing.
—GEORGE BERNARD SHAW

It takes courage to grow up and become who you really are.

—E. E. CUMMINGS

The old age of an eagle is better than the youth of a sparrow.

—GREEK PROVERB

Too many people, when they get old,

think that they have to live by the calendar.

—JOHN GLENN

After all, life hasn't much to offer except youth and

I suppose for older people the love of youth in others.

—F. SCOTT FITZGERALD

Cherish youth, but trust old age.

—NATIVE AMERICAN PROVERB

It is an illusion that youth is happy, an illusion of those who has lost it.
—W. SOMERSET MAUGHAM

It is good for a man that he bear the yoke in his youth.
—LAMENTATIONS 3:27

How old would you be if you didn't know how old you was?
—SATCHEL PAIGE

In America the young are always ready to give to those who are older
than themselves the full benefits of their inexperience.
—OSCAR WILDE

Youth gets together with their materials to build a bridge to the moon
or maybe a palace on earth; then in middle age
they decide to build a woodshed with them instead.
—HENRY DAVID THOREAU

The wine of youth does not always clear with advancing years;
sometimes it grows turbid.
— **CARL JUNG**

The great thing about getting older is that
you don't lose all the other ages you've been.
— **MADELEINE L'ENGLE**

There is a fountain of youth: it is your mind, your talents, the creativity
you bring to your life and the lives of people you love. When you learn
to tap this source, you will truly have defeated age.
— **SOPHIA LOREN**

Do not try to live forever, you will not succeed.
— **GEORGE BERNARD SHAW**

Be ashamed to die until you have won some victory for humanity.
— **HORACE MANN**

He who is of a calm and happy nature will hardly feel the
pressure of age, but to him who is of an opposite disposition,
youth and age are equally a burden.

—PLATO

At age twenty, we worry about what others think of us.
At age forty, we don't care what they think of us.
At age sixty, we discover they haven't been thinking of us at all.

—ANN LANDERS

Old age hath yet his honour and his toil.

—ALFRED, LORD TENNYSON

Grow old along with me! The best is yet to be, the last of life,
for which the first was made. Our times are in his hand who saith,
"A whole I planned, youth shows but half; Trust God:
See all, nor be afraid!"

—ROBERT BROWNING

The minute a man ceases to grow, no matter what his years,

that minute he begins to be old.

—WILLIAM JAMES

What an old man will see while seated,

a small child cannot see even standing on top of a mountain!

—NIGERIAN PROVERB

It is never too late to become what you might have been.

—GEORGE ELIOT

Old age is the most unexpected of all the things

that can happen to a man.

—JAMES THURBER

Old age is no place for sissies.

—BETTE DAVIS

Youth cannot know how age thinks and feels. But old men are
guilty if they forget what it was to be young.
—J. K. ROWLING

•

Once you're over the hill, you begin to pick up speed.
—CHARLES M. SCHULZ

•

A heart in love with beauty never grows old.
—TURKISH PROVERB

•

Age to me means nothing. I can't get old; I'm working. I was old
when I was twenty-one and out of work. As long as you're working,
you stay young. When I'm in front of an audience, all that love and
vitality sweeps over me and I forget my age.
—GEORGE BURNS

To resist the frigidity of old age, one must combine the body,

the mind, and the heart.

And to keep these in parallel vigor one must exercise,

study, and love.

—ALAN BLEASDALE

Old age does not announce itself.

—SOUTH AFRICAN PROVERB

Some day you will be old enough to start reading fairy tales again.

—C. S. LEWIS

Old age is like everything else. To make a success of it,

you've got to start young.

—THEODORE ROOSEVELT

And in the end, it's not

the years in your life that count,

it's the life in your years.

—ABRAHAM LINCOLN

You end up as you deserve. In old age you must put up with the face,
the friends, the health, and the children you have earned.
—**JUDITH VIORST**

Beautiful young people are accidents of nature,
but beautiful old people are works of art.
—**ELEANOR ROOSEVELT**

The woman who tells her age is either too young to have
anything to lose or too old to have anything to gain.
—**CHINESE PROVERB**

What most persons consider as virtue,
after the age of forty is simply a loss of energy.
—**VOLTAIRE**

The old horse in the stable still yearns to run.
—**MONGOLIAN PROVERB**

In youth the days are short and the years are long.

In old age the years are short and days long.

—POPE PAUL VI

Advice in old age is foolish; for what can be more

absurd than to increase our provisions for the road

the nearer we approach to our journey's end.

—MARCUS TULLIUS CICERO

Age is how we determine how valuable you are.

—JANE ELLIOT

Man fools himself. He prays for a long life, and he fears an old age.

—CHINESE PROVERB

I don't believe one grows older.

I think that what happens early on in life is that

at a certain age one stands still and stagnates.

—T. S. ELIOT

In old age we are like a batch of letters that someone has sent.

We are no longer in the past, we have arrived.

—KNUT HAMSUN

Old age is an excellent time for outrage. My goal is to say or do

at least one outrageous thing every week.

—LOUIS KRONENBERGER

Age is an issue of mind over matter.

If you don't mind, it doesn't matter.

—MARK TWAIN

The great secret that all old people share is that you really haven't

changed in seventy or eighty years. Your body changes,

but you don't change at all.

—DORIS LESSING

Knowledge in youth is wisdom in age.

—ENGLISH PROVERB

Old age comes on suddenly, and not gradually as is thought.
—EMILY DICKINSON

Everyone wants to live long, but no one wants to be called old.
—ICELANDIC PROVERB

I'm not interested in age.

People who tell me their age are silly.

You're as old as you feel.
—HENRI-FRÉDÉRIC AMIEL

Age is a very high price to pay for maturity.
—TOM STOPPARD

When a noble life has prepared old age,

it is not decline that it reveals, but the first days of immortality.
—MURIEL SPARK

Life is to be taken lightly by those who wish to be happy

and by those who wish to age gracefully.

—JONATHAN LOCKWOOD HUIE

You can't help getting older, but you don't have to get old.

—GEORGE BURNS

Age puzzles me.

I thought it was a quiet time.

My seventies were interesting and fairly serene,

but my eighties are passionate.

I grow more intense as I age.

—FLORIDA SCOTT-MAXWELL

An archaeologist is the best husband a woman can have.

The older she gets the more interested he is in her.

—AGATHA CHRISTIE

As I grow older, I pay less attention to what men say.

I just watch what they do.

—ANDREW CARNEGIE

•

I'm saving that rocker for the day

when I feel as old as I really am.

—DWIGHT D. EISENHOWER

•

There is an anti-aging possibility, but it has to come from within.

—SUSAN ANTON

"You are old, Father William," the young man said,

"And your hair has become very white;

And yet you incessantly stand on your head—

Do you think, at your age, it is right?"

"In my youth," Father William replied to his son,

"I feared it might injure the brain;

But, now that I'm perfectly sure I have none,

Why, I do it again and again."

"You are old," said the youth, "as I mentioned before,

And have grown most uncommonly fat;

Yet you turned a back-somersault in at the door—

Pray, what is the reason of that?"

"In my youth," said the sage, as he shook his grey locks,

"I kept all my limbs very supple

By the use of this ointment—one shilling the box—

Allow me to sell you a couple?"

"You are old," said the youth, "and your jaws are too weak
For anything tougher than suet;
Yet you finished the goose, with the bones and the beak—
Pray, how did you manage to do it?"

"In my youth," said his father, "I took to the law,
And argued each case with my wife;
And the muscular strength, which it gave to my jaw,
Has lasted the rest of my life."

"You are old," said the youth, "one would hardly suppose
That your eye was as steady as ever;
Yet you balanced an eel on the end of your nose—
What made you so awfully clever?"

"I have answered three questions, and that is enough,"
Said his father; "don't give yourself airs!
Do you think I can listen all day to such stuff?
Be off, or I'll kick you downstairs!"
—LEWIS CARROLL

Chapter

. . . .

X

On Grief and Consolation

In this sad world of ours sorrow comes to all and it often comes with
bitter agony. Perfect relief is not possible except with time. You cannot
now believe that you will ever feel better. But this is not true.
You are sure to be happy again. Knowing this, truly believing
it will make you less miserable now. I have had enough
experience to make this statement.

—ABRAHAM LINCOLN

•

Perhaps the best cure for the fear of death is to reflect that life has a
beginning as well as an end. There was a time when we were not:
this gives us no concern—why then should it trouble us
that a time will come when we shall cease to be?

—WILLIAM HAZLITT

•

As a well-spent day brings happy sleep,
so life well used brings happy death.

—LEONARDO DA VINCI

Death . . . is not more than passing from one room into another.

But there's a difference for me, you know.

Because in that other room I shall be able to see.

—HELEN KELLER

O death, where is thy sting? O grave, where is thy victory?

—1 CORINTHIANS 15:55

In the night of death, hope sees a star, and

listening love can hear the rustle of a wing.

—ROBERT INGERSOLL

Your days are short here; this is the last of your springs.

And now in the serenity and quiet of this lovely place,

touch the depths of truth, feel the hem of Heaven.

You will go away with old, good friends.

And don't forget when you leave why you came.

—ADLAI E. STEVENSON

I firmly believe that when you die you will enter
immediately into another life. They who have gone before us
are alive in one form of life and we in another.

—DR. NORMAN VINCENT PEALE

God is closest to those with broken hearts.

—JEWISH PROVERB

Do not seek death. Death will find you.
But seek the road which makes death a fulfillment.

—DAG HAMMARSKJöLD

It is foolish and wrong to mourn the men who died.
Rather we should thank God that such men lived.

—GEN. GEORGE S. PATTON JR.

Good men must die, but death cannot kill their names.

—DANISH PROVERB

Death's truer name
Is "Onward," no discordance in the roll
And march of that Eternal Harmony
Whereto the world beats time.
— **ALFRED, LORD TENNYSON**

•

Life does not cease to be funny when people die any more
than it ceases to be serious when people laugh.
— **GEORGE BERNARD SHAW**

•

That best portion of a good man's life,
His little, nameless, unremembered acts
Of kindness and of love.
— **WILLIAM WORDSWORTH**

•

There is no cure for birth and death save to enjoy the interval.
— **GEORGE SANTAYANA**

Perhaps they are not the stars, But rather openings in heaven where
The love of our lost ones pours through, and shines down upon us
to let us know they are happy.
—INUIT LEGEND

•

Death is a commingling of eternity with time;
in the death of a good man, eternity is seen looking through time.
—JOHANN WOLFGANG VON GOETHE

•

Sometimes, when one person is absent,
the whole world seems depopulated.
—ALPHONSE DE LAMARTINE

•

You can clutch the past so tightly to your chest that it leaves
your arms too full to embrace the present.
—JAN GLIDEWELL

•

God pours life into death and death into life without a drop being spilled.
—SOURCE UNKNOWN

I'm not afraid of death. It's the stake one puts up

in order to play the game of life.

— **JEAN GIRAUDOUX**

Say not in grief: "He is no more" but live in thankfulness that he was.

— **JEWISH PROVERB**

Love knows not its own depth until the hour of separation.

— **KAHLIL GIBRAN**

Just as a little bird cracks open the shell and flies out, we fly out of this

shell, the shell of the body. We call that death, but strictly speaking,

death is nothing but a change of form.

— **SWAMI SATCHIDANANDA**

The family exists for many reasons, but its most basic function

may be to draw together after a member dies.

— **STEPHEN KING**

A death is not the extinguishing of a light,

but the putting out of the lamp because the dawn has come . . .

Let the dead have the immortality of fame,

but the living the immortality of love.

—RABINDANRATH TAGORE

•

Let us endeavor to live so that when we come to die

even the undertaker will be sorry.

—MARK TWAIN

•

Don't cry because it's over. Smile because it happened.

—DR. SEUSS (THEODORE GEISEL)

•

While we are mourning the loss of our friend, others are rejoicing to

meet him behind the veil.

—JOHN TAYLOR

He who has gone, so we but cherish his memory, abides with us,
more potent, nay, more present than the living man.
—ANTOINE DE SAINT-EXUPÉRY

The greatest thing in life is to die young but to take as long
a time as possible to do it.
—GEORGE BERNARD SHAW

We must embrace pain and burn it as fuel for our journey.
—KENJI MIYAZAWA

Death is a challenge. It tells us not to waste time. . . .
It tells us to tell each other right now that we love each other.
—LEO BUSCAGLIA

To live in hearts we leave behind is not to die.
—CLYDE CAMPBELL

If you suppress grief too much, it can well redouble.
—MOLIÈRE

Only in the agony of parting do we look into the depths of love.
—GEORGE ELIOT

Let children walk with Nature, let them see the beautiful
blendings and communions of death and life, their joyous inseparable
unity, as taught in woods and meadows, plains and mountains and
streams of our blessed star, and they will learn that death is
stingless indeed, and as beautiful as life.
—JOHN MUIR

The joy in life is to be used for a purpose.
I want to be used up when I die.
—GEORGE BERNARD SHAW

For death is no more than a turning of us over from time to eternity.
—WILLIAM PENN

The courage of life is often a less dramatic spectacle
than the courage of the final moment; but it is no less
a magnificent mixture of triumph and tragedy.
— **JOHN F. KENNEDY**

•

Good-night! good-night! as we so oft have said
Beneath this roof at midnight, in the days
That are no more, and shall no more return.
Thou hast but taken up thy lamp and gone to bed;
I stay a little longer, as one stays
To cover up the embers that still burn.
— **HENRY WADSWORTH LONGFELLOW**

•

Let yourself be inert, wait till the incomprehensible power . . . that has
broken you restores you a little, I say a little, for henceforth you will
always keep something broken about you. Tell yourself this, too, for it
is a kind of pleasure to know that you will never love less, that you will
never be consoled, that you will constantly remember more and more.
— **MARCEL PROUST**

Unable are the Loved to die/For Love is Immortality.
—EMILY DICKINSON

•

Our fear of death is like our fear that summer will be short,
but when we have had our swing of pleasure, our fill of fruit, and
our swelter of heat, we say we have had our day.
—RALPH WALDO EMERSON

•

Expect trouble as an inevitable part of life and repeat to yourself,
the most comforting words of all: This, too, shall pass.
—ANN LANDERS

•

Death leaves a heartache no one can heal,
love leaves a memory no one can steal.
—AN IRISH TOMBSTONE EPITAPH

•

In sorrow we must go, but not in despair.
Behold! We are not bound for ever to the circles of the world, and
beyond them is more than memory.
—J. R. TOLKIEN

What soap is for the body, tears are for the soul.
— **JEWISH PROVERB**

To everything there is a season and a time for every purpose
under heaven. A time to be born, and a time to die . . .
— **ECCLESIASTES 3:1**

Give sorrow words; the grief that does not speak
knits up the o'er wrought heart and bids it break.
— **WILLIAM SHAKESPEARE**

Life is but a journey; death is returning home.
— **CHINESE PROVERB**

My feet will want to walk to where you are sleeping,
But I shall go on living.
— **PABLO NERUDA**

As a well spent day brings happy sleep,

so a life well spent brings happy death.

—LEONARDO DA VINCI

•

Though lovers be lost, love shall not;

And death shall have no dominion.

—DYLAN THOMAS

•

For everything that was written in the past was written to teach us,

so that through the endurance taught in the Scriptures and

the encouragement they provide we might have hope.

—ROMANS 15:4

•

Absence is a house so vast that inside you will pass through its walls

and hang pictures on the air.

—PABLO NERUDA

•

Blessed are those who mourn, for they will be comforted.

—MATTHEW 5:4

As long as we live, they too will live; for they are now are a part of us;

as we remember them.

—HEBREW PRAYER

Or even the silver cord be loosed, or the golden bowl be broken,

or the pitcher be broken at the cistern.

Then shall the dust return to the earth as it was,

and the spirit shall return to God who gave it.

—ECCLESIASTES 12:7

Question me now about all other matters, but do not ask who I am, for

fear you may increase in my heart its burden of sorrow as I think back;

I am very full of grief, and I should not sit in the house of somebody

else with my lamentation and wailing. It is not good to go on

mourning forever.

—HOMER

Earth has no sorrow that Heaven can't heal.

—SOURCE UNKNOWN

When you are sorrowful look again in your heart, and you shall see
that in truth you are weeping for that which has been your delight.
—KAHLIL GIBRAN

•

The "gift" of grief is that it presents us with
the opportunity to heal and grow.
—JEWISH PROVERB

•

To hold, you must first open your hand. Let go.
—TAO TE CHING

•

Grief is like the ocean; it comes on waves ebbing and flowing.
Sometimes the water is calm, and sometimes it is overwhelming.
All we can do is learn to swim.
—VICKI HARRISON

•

Death ends a life, not a relationship.
—MORRIE SCHWARTZ

Goodbyes are not forever. Goodbyes are not the end.

They simply mean I'll miss you.

Until we meet again!

— SOURCE UNKNOWN

●

There is a sacredness in tears. They are not the mark of weakness, but

of power. They speak more eloquently than ten thousand tongues.

They are messengers of overwhelming grief . . . and unspeakable love.

— WASHINGTON IRVING

●

Death is nothing else but going home to God,

the bond of love will be unbroken for all eternity.

— MOTHER TERESA

●

Don't be dismayed at goodbyes, a farewell is necessary before you can

meet again and meeting again, after moments or lifetimes,

is certain for those who are friends.

— RICHARD BACH

Death is simply a shedding of the physical body like the butterfly shedding its cocoon. It is a transition to a higher state of consciousness where you continue to perceive, to understand, to laugh, and to be able to grow.

—ELISABETH KÜBLER-ROSS, M.D.

•

I experienced the reality of the spiritual body and learned that it has every faculty of the physical body, though with greater sensitivity and some dimensions added. . . . There will be nothing shocking in the transition, only a continuation of who I am now.

—CATHERINE MARSHALL

•

Death is not the end, it is simply walking out of the physical form and into the spirit realm, which is our true home. It's going back home.

—STEPHEN CHRISTOPHER

I am quite confident that the most important part of a human being is not his physical body but his nonphysical essence, which some people call soul and others, personality. . . . The nonphysical part cannot die and cannot decay because it's not physical.

—RABBI HAROLD KUSHNER

●

He spake well who said that graves are the footprints of angels.

—HENRY WADSWORTH LONGFELLOW

●

A human life is a story told by God.

—HANS CHRISTIAN ANDERSEN

●

You lose a parent, you suddenly realize what a slender thing life is, how easily you can lose those you love. Then out of that comes a new simplicity and that is why sometimes all the pain and the tears lift you to a much higher and deeper joy when you say to the bad times, "I will not let you go until you bless me."

—RABBI JONATHAN SACKS

Music, when soft voices die,

Vibrates in the memory;

Odours, when sweet violets sicken,

Live within the sense they quicken.

Rose leaves, when the rose is dead,

Are heap'd for the beloved's bed;

And so thy thoughts, when thou art gone,

Love itself shall slumber on.

—PERCY BYSSHE SHELLEY

Remember me when I am gone away,

Gone far away into the silent land;

When you can no more hold me by the hand,

Nor I half turn to go, yet turning stay.

Remember me when no more day by day

You tell me of our future that you plann'd:

Only remember me; you understand

It will be late to counsel then or pray.

Yet if you should forget me for a while

And afterwards remember, do not grieve:

For if the darkness and corruption leave

A vestige of the thoughts that once I had,

Better by far you should forget and smile

Than that you should remember and be sad.

—CHRISTINA ROSSETTI

But when ye come, and all the flowers are dying,

If I am dead, as dead I well may be,

You'll come and find the place where I am lying,

And kneel and say *Ave* there for me,

And I shall hear, though soft you tread above me,

And all my grave will warmer, sweeter be,

For you will bend and tell me that you love me,

And I shall sleep in peace until you come to me.

— "DANNY BOY"

Chapter

· · · · · · · · · · ·

XI

On Education

Education is not to reform students or amuse them or to make them expert technicians. It is to unsettle their minds, widen their horizons, inflame their intellects, teach them to think straight, if possible.
—ROBERT M. HUTCHINS

Education is our only political safety. Outside of this ark, all is deluge.
—HORACE MANN

Does America have the will to make education a priority? We know the things that work. Why don't we scale up those things that do work.
—TAVIS SMILEY

Give a man a fish and you have fed him for a day.
Teach a man to fish and you have fed him for a lifetime.
—CHINESE PROVERB

It is easier to build strong children than to repair broken men.
—FREDERICK DOUGLASS

When you lose, don't lose the lesson.

—**SOURCE UNKNOWN**

What we want to see is the child in pursuit of the knowledge
not the knowledge in pursuit of the child.

—**GEORGE BERNARD SHAW**

My alma mater was books, a good library . . . I could spend the
rest of my life reading, just satisfying my curiosity.

—**MALCOLM X**

A good book is the best of friends, the same today and forever.

—**MARTIN FARQUAR TUPPER**

A scoffer seeks wisdom in vain, but knowledge is easy for
a man of understanding. Leave the presence of a fool,
for there you do not meet words of knowledge.

—**PROVERBS 14:6-7**

Do not train a child to learn by force or harshness; but direct them to it by what amuses their minds, so that you may be better able to discover with accuracy the peculiar bent of the genius of each.

— PLATO

In a library we are surrounded by many hundreds of dear friends imprisoned by an enchanter in paper and leathern boxes.

— RALPH WALDO EMERSON

The mind is not a vessel to be filled but a fire to be kindled.

— PLUTARCH

In questions of science, the authority of a thousand is not worth the humble reasoning of a single individual.

— GALILEO GALILEI

The advancement and diffusion of knowledge is the only guardian of true liberty.

— JAMES MADISON

Tell me and I'll forget. Show me, and I may not remember.
Involve me, and I'll understand.
—**NATIVE AMERICAN PROVERB**

●

The beautiful thing about learning is that no one
can take it away from you.
—**B. B. KING**

●

For things that we have to learn before we can do them,
we learn by doing them.
—**ARISTOTLE**

●

What we learn with pleasure we never forget.
—**ALFRED MERCIER**

●

Education is simply the soul of a society as it passes
from one generation to another.
—**G. K. CHESTERTON**

Instruction ends in the schoolroom, but education ends only with life.
—FREDERICK M. ROBERTSON

•

I have never let my schooling interfere with my education.
—MARK TWAIN

•

It is impossible for a man to learn what he thinks he already knows.
—EPICTETUS

•

Education costs money, but then so does ignorance.
—CLAUS MOSER

Have you ever been at sea in a dense fog, when it seemed as if a
tangible white darkness shut you in and the great ship, tense and
anxious, groped her way toward the shore with plummet and sounding-
line, and you waited with beating heart for something to happen? I was
like that ship before my education began, only I was without compass
or sounding-line, and no way of knowing how near the harbor was.
Light! Give me light! was the wordless cry of my soul, and
the light of love shone on me in that very hour.
—HELEN KELLER

You can teach a student a lesson for a day;
but if you can teach him to learn by creating curiosity,
he will continue the learning process as long as he lives.
—CLAY P. BEDFORD

A teacher affects eternity; he can never tell where his influence stops.
—HENRY B. ADAMS

The first problem for all of us, men and women,

is not to learn, but to unlearn.

— GLORIA STEINEM

Children have never been very good at listening to their elders,

but they have never failed to imitate them.

— JAMES BALDWIN

A scholar is just a library's way of making another library.

— DANIEL DENNETT

Education is a progressive discovery of our own ignorance.

— WILL DURANT

If someone is going down the wrong road, he doesn't need motivation

to speed him up. What he needs is education to turn him around.

— JIM ROHN

People learn something every day, and a lot of times it's
that what they learned the day before was wrong.
— **BILL VAUGHAN**

What sculpture is to a block of marble education is to the human soul.
— **JOSEPH ADDISON**

Education makes a people easy to lead but difficult to drive:
easy to govern, but impossible to enslave.
— **PETER BROUGHAM**

When the student is ready, the teacher will appear.
— **BUDDHIST PROVERB**

Do not train children to learning by force and harshness, but direct
them to it by what amuses their minds, so that you may be better able
to discover with accuracy the peculiar bent of the genius of each.
— **PLATO**

If people did not do silly things, nothing intelligent would ever get done.
—LUDWIG WITTGENSTEIN

It is in fact a part of the function of education to help us escape,
not from our own time—for we are bound by that—but from the
intellectual and emotional limitations of our time.
—T. S. ELIOT

Whatever is good to know is difficult to learn.
—GREEK PROVERB

Education is the ability to listen to almost anything without losing
your temper or your self-confidence.
—ROBERT FROST

Learning is not attained by chance, it must be sought for
with ardor and attended to with diligence.
—ABIGAIL ADAMS

To teach is to learn twice.
—JOSEPH JOUBERT

What we have learned from others becomes our own reflection.
—RALPH WALDO EMERSON

The best and most important part of every man's education
is that which he gives himself.
—EDWARD GIBBON

Education is the key to unlock the golden door of freedom.
—GEORGE WASHINGTON CARVER

If a nation expects to be ignorant and free, in a state of civilization,
it expects what never was and will never be.
—THOMAS JEFFERSON

It is a greater work to educate a child, in the true and
larger sense of the word, than to rule a state.
—**WILLIAM ELLERY CHANNING**

It is a greater work to educate a child, in the true and

Learning is the only thing the mind never exhausts,
never fears, and never regrets.
—**LEONARDO DA VINCI**

Education is more than a luxury;
it is a responsibility that society owes to itself.
—**ROBIN COOK**

Let us never be betrayed into saying we have finished our education;
because that would mean we had stopped growing.
—**JULIA H. GULLIVER**

The fruit of liberal education is not learning, but the capacity and
desire to learn, not knowledge, but power.
—**CHARLES W. ELIOT**

The ultimate goal of the educational system is to shift to the
individual the burden of pursuing his education.
—**JOHN W. GARDNER**

Intelligence plus character—that is the goal of true education.
—**MARTIN LUTHER KING JR.**

I am still learning.
—**MICHELANGELO DI LODOVICO BUONARROTI SIMONI**

You can get help from teachers, but you are going to have to
learn a lot by yourself, sitting alone in a room.
—**DR. SEUSS (THEODORE GEISEL)**

Next in importance to freedom and justice is popular education,
without which neither freedom nor justice can be maintained.
—**JAMES A. GARFIELD**

Emeralds as well as glass will shine when the light is shed on them.
—**JAPANESE PROVERB**

•

Education, like the mass of our age's inventions, is after all, only a tool;
everything depends upon the workman who uses it.
—**CHARLES WAGNER**

•

Learning is like rowing upstream: not to advance is to drop back.
—**CHINESE PROVERB**

•

Education should bring to light the ideal of the individual.
—**JOHANN PAUL FRIEDRICH RICHTER**

•

Education should consist of a series of enchantments,
each raising the individual to a higher level of awareness,
understanding, and kinship with all living things.
—**SOURCE UNKNOWN**

When asked how much educated men were
superior to those uneducated, Aristotle answered,
"As much as the living are to the dead."
—**DIOGENES LAERTIUS**

Upon the education of the people of this country,
the fate of this country depends.
—**BENJAMIN DISRAELI**

Education is the best provision for old age.
—**ARISTOTLE**

Live as if you were to die tomorrow. Learn as if you were to live forever.
—**MOHANDAS GANDHI**

Do not wait to strike till the iron is hot; but make it hot by striking.
—**WILLIAM BUTLER YEATS**

Learning is not a spectator sport.
—**AMERICAN PROVERB**

It is wiser to find out than to suppose.
—**MARK TWAIN**

Learn from yesterday, live for today, hope for tomorrow.
—**ALBERT EINSTEIN**

The purpose of learning is growth, and our minds, unlike our bodies,
can continue growing as long as we live.
—**MORTIMER ADLER**

Be a student as long as you still have something to learn,
and this will mean all your life.
—**HENRY L. DOHERTY**

What we become depends on what we read after all the professors have finished with us. The greatest university of all is a collection of books.
—**THOMAS CARLYLE**

Being a role model is the most powerful form of educating. Youngsters need good models more than they need critics.
—**JOHN WOODEN**

Education is our passport to the future, for tomorrow belongs to the people who prepare for it today.
—**MALCOLM X**

To educate a person in mind and not in morals is to educate a menace to society.
—**THEODORE ROOSEVELT**

Education is what survives when what has been learned has been forgotten.
—**B. F. SKINNER**

Chapter

· · · · · · · · · · ·

XII

On Faith

Faith is a grand cathedral, with divinely pictured windows—standing without, you can see no glory, nor can you imagine any, but standing within every ray of light reveals a harmony of unspeakable splendors.
—NATHANIEL HAWTHORNE

In our sleep, pain which cannot forget falls drop by drop upon the heart until in our own despair against our will comes wisdom through the awful grace of God.
—AESCHYLUS

Faith is the substance of things hoped for,
the evidence of things not seen.
—HEBREWS 11:1

Someday, after mastering the winds, the waves, the tides and gravity, we shall harness for God the energies of love, and then, for a second time in the history of the world, man will have discovered fire.
—PIERRE TEILHARD DE CHARDIN

I prayed for twenty years but received no answer
until I prayed with my legs.
—FREDERICK DOUGLASS

Let us have faith that right makes might, and in that faith,
let us, to the end, dare to do our duty as we understand it.
—ABRAHAM LINCOLN

The reason birds can fly and we can't is simply because they
have perfect faith, for to have faith is to have wings.
—SIR JAMES M. BARRIE

My religion consists of a humble admiration of the illimitable
superior spirit who reveals himself in the slight details
we are able to perceive with our frail and feeble mind.
—ALBERT EINSTEIN

The only faith that wears well and holds its color in all weathers,

is that which is woven of conviction and set with

the sharp mordant of experience.

—JAMES RUSSELL LOWELL

•

Optimism is the faith that leads to achievement.

Nothing can be done without hope and confidence.

—HELEN KELLER

•

The antidote to frustration is a calm faith, not in your own cleverness,

or in hard toil, but in God's guidance.

—NORMAN VINCENT PEALE

•

Faith is not a complex set of theological propositions. It is simpler and

deeper than that. It is about not taking things for granted.

It is a sustained discipline of meditation on the miracle of being.

—RABBI JONATHAN SACKS

This is what the Lord asks of you: only this,

to act justly, to love tenderly,

and to walk humbly with your God.

—MICAH 6:8

Faith allows things to happen. It is the power that comes from a
fearless heart. And when a fearless heart believes, miracles happen.

—SOURCE UNKNOWN

You must not lose faith in humanity. Humanity is like an ocean; if a
few drops of the ocean are dirty, the ocean does not become dirty.

—MOHANDAS GANDHI

Lord, I'm going to hold steady on to You and

You've got to see me through.

—HARRIET TUBMAN

I believe in everything until it's disproved. So I believe in fairies, the myths, dragons. It all exists, even if it's in your mind. Who's to say that dreams and nightmares aren't as real as the here and now?

—JOHN LENNON

To fear is to expect punishment. To love is to know we are immersed, not in darkness, but in light.

—MOTHER TERESA

Without faith a man can do nothing; with it all things are possible.

—SIR WILLIAM OSLER

Three things are necessary for the salvation of man:
to know what he ought to believe; to know what he ought to desire;
and to know what he ought to do.

—ST. THOMAS AQUINAS

The heart that is generous and kind most resembles God.

—ROBERT BURNS

All I have seen teaches me to trust the Creator for all I have not seen.
—**RALPH WALDO EMERSON**

Fear knocked at the door and faith answered. No one was there.
—**ENGLISH PROVERB**

Lord, grand that I might not so much seek to be loved as to love.
—**ST. FRANCIS OF ASSISI**

Call no faith false which e'er hath brought

Relief to any laden life,

Cessation to the pain of thought,

Refreshment mid the dust of strife.
—**SIR LEWIS MORRIS**

I have never made but one prayer to God,

a very short one: "O Lord make my enemies ridiculous."

And God granted it.
—**VOLTAIRE**

Giving is more than a responsibility—it is a privilege;

more than an act of obedience—it is evidence of our faith.

—WILLIAM ARTHUR WARD

•

We are not human beings having a spiritual experience.

We are spiritual beings having a human experience.

—ATTRIBUTED TO PIERRE TEILHARD DE CHARDIN

•

We walk by faith, not by sight.

—2 CORINTHIANS 7

•

And 'tis my faith, that every flower

Enjoys the air it breathes.

—WILLIAM WORDSWORTH

•

Do not be afraid; our fate

Cannot be taken from us; it is a gift.

—DANTE ALIGHIERI

There were many dark moments when my faith in humanity was sorely
tested, but I would not and could not give myself up to despair.
That way lays defeat and death.
—**NELSON MANDELA**

•

Charity may be a very short word, but with its tremendous meaning of
pure love, it sums up man's entire relation to God and to his neighbor.
—**ST. AELRED OF RIEVAULX**

•

Faith is to believe what you do not yet see;
the reward for this faith is to see what you believe.
—**SAINT AUGUSTINE**

•

The majesty of faith is that it teaches us to see what exists,
not merely what catches our attention.
—**RABBI JONATHAN SACKS**

. . . my sole concern has been to save myself by work and faith.

—JEAN-PAUL SARTRE

When faith is lost, when honor dies,

The man is dead!

—JOHN GREENLEAF WHITTIER

To be pleased at correction and reproofs shows that one loves the virtues which are contrary to those faults for which he is corrected and reproved. And, therefore, it is a great sign of advancement in perfection.

—ST. FRANCIS DE SALES

There lives more faith in honest doubt,

Believe me, than in half the creeds.

—ALFRED, LORD TENNYSON

Give me my scallop-shell of quiet,

My staff of faith to walk upon,

My scrip of joy, immortal diet,

My bottle of salvation,

My gown of glory, hope's true gage;

And thus I'll take my pilgrimage.

—SIR WALTER RALEIGH

Chapter

XIII

On Law and Justice

The only stable state is the one in which all men are equal before the law.
—ARISTOTLE

•

Human progress is neither automatic nor inevitable. . . . Every step toward the goal of justice requires sacrifice, suffering, and struggle; the tireless exertions and passionate concern of dedicated individuals.
—MARTIN LUTHER KING JR.

•

Justice will not be served until those who are unaffected are as outraged as those who are.
—BENJAMIN FRANKLIN

•

Revolution is about the need to re-evolve political, economic, and social justice and power back into the hands of the people, preferably through legislation and policies that make human sense.
—BOBBY SEALE

•

It is not desirable to cultivate a respect for the law, so much as for the right.
—HENRY DAVID THOREAU

We must not make a scarecrow of the law,

Setting it up to fear the birds of prey,

And let it keep one shape, till custom make it.

Their perch and not their terror.

—WILLIAM SHAKESPEARE

•

Laws are made to instruct the good, and in the hope that

there may be no need of them; also to control the bad,

whose hardness of heart will not be hindered from crime.

—PLATO

•

In any event, mere speed is not a test of justice. Deliberate speed is.

Deliberate speed takes time. But it is time well spent.

FELIX FRANKFURTER

•

The good of the people is the chief law.

—CICERO

We must reject the idea that every time a law's broken, society is guilty rather than the lawbreaker. It is time to restore the American precept that each individual is accountable for his actions.
—RONALD REAGAN

Justice is truth in action.
—BENJAMIN DISRAELI

No man is above the law and no man is below it;
nor do we ask any man's permission when we ask him to obey it.
Obedience to the law is demanded as a right; not asked as a favor.
—THEODORE ROOSEVELT

Justice, sir, is the great interest of man on earth.
—DANIEL WEBSTER

The life of the law has not been logic; it has been reason.
—OLIVER WENDELL HOLMES JR.

You cannot make men good by law: and without good men
you cannot have a good society.
—C. S. LEWIS

•

As long as I have any choice, I will stay only in a country
where political liberty, toleration, and equality of all citizens
before the law are the rule.
—ALBERT EINSTEIN

•

Justice that love gives is a surrender,
justice that law gives is a punishment.
—MOHANDAS GANDHI

•

Shame may restrain what law does not prohibit.
—SENECA

•

What is hateful to thyself do not do to another.
That is the whole Torah [Law], the rest is commentary.
—HILLEL THE ELDER

The best way to get a bad law repealed is to enforce it strictly.
—ABRAHAM LINCOLN

•

A country is in a bad state, which is governed only by laws;
because a thousand things occur for which laws cannot provide,
and where authority ought to interpose.
—SAMUEL JOHNSON

•

Law and justice are not always the same.
—GLORIA STEINEM

•

Truth is its [justice's] handmaid, freedom is its child, peace is its
companion, safety walks in its steps, victory follows in its train;
it is the brightest emanation from the Gospel;
it is the attribute of God.
—SYDNEY SMITH

•

It is the spirit and not the form of law that keeps justice alive.
—EARL WARREN

In matters of truth and justice, there is no difference
between large and small problems, for issues concerning
the treatment of people are all the same.
—**ALBERT EINSTEIN**

Many laws as certainly make bad men, as bad men make many laws.
—**WALTER SAVAGE LANDOR**

Why should there not be a patient confidence in the ultimate justice of
the people? Is there any better or equal hope in the world?
—**ABRAHAM LINCOLN**

Punishment is now unfashionable . . . because it creates moral
distinctions among men, which, to the democratic mind,
are odious. We prefer a meaningless collective guilt to a
meaningful individual responsibility.
—**THOMAS SZASZ**

Bad laws are the worst sort of tyranny.
—**EDMUND BURKE**

I'm convinced that every boy, in his heart,

would rather steal second base than an automobile.

—TOM CLARK

Revenge is a kind of wild justice, which the more man's nature runs to,

the more ought law to weed it out.

—SIR FRANCIS BACON

The law, in its majestic equality, forbids the rich as well as the poor to

sleep under bridges, to beg in the streets, and to steal bread.

—ANATOLE FRANCE

Corn can't expect justice from a court composed of chickens.

—AFRICAN PROVERB

Rather let the crime of the guilty go unpunished

than condemn the innocent.

—JUSTINIAN

The law embodies the story of a nation's development through many centuries, and it cannot be dealt with as if it contained only the axioms and corollaries of a book of mathematics.

—OLIVER WENDELL HOLMES JR.

•

Fill the seats of justice

With good men, not so absolute in goodness

As to forget what human frailty is.

—SIR THOMAS TALFOURD

•

Man, when perfected, is the best of animals, but when separated from law and justice, he is the worst of all.

—ARISTOTLE

•

He [Aristotle] used to define justice as "a virtue of the soul distributing that which each person deserved."

—DIOGENES LAERTIUS

The law "an eye for an eye" makes the whole world blind.

— **MOHANDAS GANDHI**

Whereas the law is passionless, passion must ever sway the heart of man.

—**ARISTOTLE**

Where law ends, there tyranny begins.

—**WILLIAM PITT THE ELDER**

A state is better governed which has few laws, and those laws strictly observed.

—**RENÉ DESCARTES**

Laws alone cannot secure freedom of expression;
in order that every man present his views without penalty
there must be spirit of tolerance in the entire population.

—**ALBERT EINSTEIN**

Laws are not masters but servants, and he rules them who obeys them.

—HENRY WARD BEECHER

The good need fear no law; it is his safety, and the bad man's awe.

—BEN JONSON

Let every man remember that to violate the law is
to trample on the blood of his father, and to tear that
charter of his own and his children's liberty.

—ABRAHAM LINCOLN

Nobody has a more sacred obligation to obey the law
than those who make the law.

—SOPHOCLES

But the sunshine aye shall light the sky,

As round and round we run;

And the truth shall ever come uppermost,

And justice shall be done.

—CHARLES MACKAY

The quality of mercy is not strain'd,

It droppeth as the gentle rain from heaven

Upon the place beneath. It is twice blest:

It blesseth him that gives and him that takes.

—WILLIAM SHAKESPEARE

Chapter

· · · · · · · · · · · ·

XIV

On Leisure

To be able to fill leisure intelligently is the last product of civilization.

—**ARNOLD J. TOYNBEE**

The end of labor is to gain leisure.

—**ARISTOTLE**

Idleness, like kisses, to be sweet must be stolen.

—**JEROME K. JEROME**

My father taught me to work, but not to love it. I never did like to work, and I don't deny it. I'd rather read, tell stories, crack jokes, talk, laugh—anything but work.

—**ABRAHAM LINCOLN**

There can be no high civilization where there is not ample leisure.

—**HENRY WARD BEECHER**

Rest is the sauce of labor.

—**PLUTARCH**

There are moments when all anxiety and stated toil are becalmed
in the infinite leisure and repose of nature.
— HENRY DAVID THOREAU

Two weeks ago I went into retirement. Am I glad that's over!
It took all the fun out of Saturdays.
— RONALD REAGAN

If you are losing your leisure, look out; you may be losing your soul.
— LOGAN P. SMITH

It is in his pleasure that a man really lives; it is from his leisure that he
constructs the true fabric of self.
— AGNES REPPLIER

When a man's busy, why, leisure
Strikes him as wonderful pleasure:
Faith, and at leisure once is he?
Straightway he wants to be busy.
— ROBERT BROWNING

The supreme accomplishment is to blur the line between work and play.

—ARNOLD J. TOYNBEE

•

Wisdom and penetration are the fruit of experience,

not the lessons of retirement and leisure.

Great necessities call out great virtues.

—ABIGAIL ADAMS

•

The busier we are, the more leisure we have.

—WILLIAM HAZLITT

•

They talk of the dignity of work.

The dignity is in leisure.

—HERMAN MELVILLE

•

He hath no leisure who useth it not.

—GEORGE HERBERT

The best intelligence test is what we do with our leisure.
—**LAURENCE J. PETER**

In itself and in its consequences the life of leisure
is beautiful and ennobling in all civilised men's eyes.
—**THORSTEIN VEBLEN**

Friendship requires more time than poor busy men
can usually command.
—**RALPH WALDO EMERSON**

The soul is dyed with the color of its leisure thoughts.
—**WILLIAM RALPH "DEAN" INGE**

One cannot rest except after steady practice.
—**GEORGE ADE**

O, blest retirement! friend to life's decline—

How blest is he who crowns, in shades like these,

A youth of labor with an age of ease!

—OLIVER GOLDSMITH

Increased means and increased leisure are the two civilizers of man.

—BENJAMIN DISRAELI

The primary purpose of a liberal education is to make

one's mind a pleasant place in which to spend one's leisure.

—SYDNEY J. HARRIS

In our leisure we reveal what kind of people we are.

—OVID

What we do during our working hours determines what we have;

what we do in our leisure hours determines what we are.

—GEORGE EASTMAN

Friendship is a very taxing and arduous form of leisure activity.
— **MORTIMER ADLER**

No president who performs his duties faithfully and

conscientiously can have any leisure.
— **JAMES K. POLK**

If you are losing your leisure, look out; you may be losing your soul.
— **LOGAN P. SMITH**

Leisure is the Mother of Philosophy.
— **THOMAS HOBBES**

The more we do, the more we can do; the more busy we are,

the more leisure we have.
— **DAG HAMMARSKJÖLD**

Those who decide to use leisure as a means of mental development,

who love good music, good books, good pictures,

good plays, good company, good conversation—

what are they? They are the happiest people in the world.

—WILLIAM LYON PHELPS

All happiness depends on a leisurely breakfast.

—JOHN GUNTHER

Work is not always required. There is such a thing as sacred idleness.

—GEORGE MACDONALD

It takes application, a fine sense of value,

and a powerful community-spirit for a people to have serious leisure,

and this has not been the genius of the Americans.

—PAUL GOODMAN

Don't simply retire from something; have something to retire to.

—HARRY EMERSON FOSDICK

Horas non numero nisi serenus [translation: "I count only the serene hours"]—is the motto of a sundial near Venice. There is a softness and a harmony in the words and in the thought unparalleled.

—WILLIAM HAZLITT

A man can never be idle with safety and advantage until he has been so trained by work that he makes his freedom from times and tasks more fruitful than his toil has been.

—HAMILTON WRIGHT MAYBIE

I would not exchange my leisure hours for all the wealth in the world.

—COMTE DE MIRABEAU

Guard well your spare moments. They are like uncut diamonds. Discard them and their value will never be known. Improve them and they will become the brightest gems in a useful life.

—RALPH WALDO EMERSON

In itself and in its consequences the life of leisure is beautiful and
ennobling in all civilised men's eyes.
—THORSTEIN VEBLEN

There's never enough time to do all the nothing you want.
—BILL WATTERSON
(IN HIS "CALVIN AND HOBBES" COMIC STRIP)

The real problem of leisure time is how to keep others from using yours.
—ARTHUR LACEY

We give up leisure in order that we may have leisure,
just as we go to war in order that we may have peace.
—ARISTOTLE

Leisure and curiosity might soon make great advances in
useful knowledge, were they not diverted by
minute emulation and laborious trifles.
—SAMUEL JOHNSON

Leisure can be both a problem and a solution.
—**NATHANIEL LETONNERRE**

Leisure is a beautiful garment, but it will not do for constant wear.
—**SOURCE UNKNOWN**

Leisure only means a chance to do other jobs that demand attention
—**OLIVER WENDELL HOLMES JR.**

There are days in retirement that are the waking equivalent of a
dreamless sleep, if you know what I mean.
—**ROBERT BRAULT**

When a habit begins to cost money, it's called a hobby.
—**JEWISH PROVERB**

Lie down and listen to the crabgrass grow The faucet leak,

and learn to leave them so.

—MARYA MANNES

•

He enjoys true leisure who has time to improve his soul's estate.

—HENRY DAVID THOREAU

Chapter

· · · · · · · · · · ·

XV

On Success at Sports

Never say never because limits, like fears, are often just an illusion.

—**MICHAEL JORDAN**

•

The strength of the group is the strength of the leaders.

—**VINCE LOMBARDI**

•

Health, happiness, and success depend upon the fighting spirit of
each person. The big thing is not what happens to us in life—
but what we do about what happens to us.

—**GEORGE ALLEN**

•

You can become a winner only if you are willing to walk over the edge.

—**DAMON RUNYON**

•

If you are going to be a champion, you must be willing to pay a greater price.

—**BUD WILKINSON**

•

Never mistake activity for achievement.

—**JOHN WOODEN**

Desire is the key to motivation, but it's the determination and commitment to an unrelenting pursuit of your goal—a commitment to excellence—that will enable you to attain the success you seek.
—MARIO ANDRETTI

Every time you stay out late; every time you sleep in; every time you miss a workout; every time you don't give 100% . . . you make it that much easier for me to beat you.
—SIGN ON MANY LOCKER-ROOM WALLS

The man who can drive himself further once the effort gets painful is the man who will win.
—ROGER BANNISTER

It's a funny thing, the more I practice the luckier I get.
—ARNOLD PALMER

Inside of a ring or out, ain't nothing wrong with going down. It's staying down that's wrong.
—MUHAMMAD ALI

Excellence is being the best you can be.
—MIKE DITKA

The harder you work, the harder it is to surrender.
—VINCE LOMBARDI

You can't make a great play unless you do it first in practice.
—CHUCK NOLL

Never let your head hang down.
Never give up and sit down and grieve. Find another way.
—SATCHEL PAIGE

Things that hurt, instruct.
—BENJAMIN FRANKLIN

Everybody pulls for David, nobody roots for Goliath.
—WILT CHAMBERLAIN

One man can be a crucial ingredient on a team,

but one man cannot make a team.

—KAREEM ABDUL-JABBAR

*

When I was young, I never wanted to leave the court until I got

things exactly correct. My dream was to become a pro.

—LARRY BIRD

*

My responsibility is getting all my players playing for the name on

the front of the jersey, not the one on the back.

—SOURCE UNKNOWN

*

Good, better, best. Never let it rest.

Until your good is better and your better is best.

—TIM DUNCAN

*

You owe it to yourself to be the best you can

possibly be in baseball and in life.

—PETE ROSE

It takes a lot of hard work and dedication just like any pro sport.
Especially for beach volleyball you don't have to be tall or as fast as
other sports. You just have to have the skills.
—MISTY MAY-TREANOR

Make sure that team members know they are working with you, not for you.
—JOHN WOODEN

Leadership, like coaching, is fighting for the hearts and souls of men
and getting them to believe in you.
—EDDIE ROBINSON

What makes a good coach? Complete dedication.
—GEORGE HALAS

I learn teaching from teachers. I learn golf from golfers.
I learn winning from coaches.
—HARVEY PENICK

You can motivate by fear, and you can motivate by reward.

But both those methods are only temporary.

The only lasting thing is self-motivation.

—HOMER RICE

●

My responsibility is leadership, and the minute I get negative,

that is going to have an influence on my team.

—DON SHULA

●

In the end, the game comes down to one thing: man against man.

May the best man win.

—SAM HUFF

●

Every game is an opportunity to measure yourself against

your own potential.

—BUD WILKINSON

●

It is how you show up at the showdown that counts.

—HOMER NORTON

Without self-discipline, success is impossible, period.
—**LOU HOLTZ**

If you aren't going all the way, why go at all?
—**JOE NAMATH**

If you don't practice you don't deserve to win.
—**ANDRE AGASSI**

Winning isn't everything, but wanting to win is.
—**VINCE LOMBARDI**

Maybe the day will come when I can sit back and be content. . . .
But until that day comes, I intend to stay in the batter's box—
I don't let the big guys push me out of there anymore—
and keep hammering away.
—**HANK AARON**

Most ball games are lost, not won.
—**CASEY STENGEL**

It isn't hard to be good from time to time in sports.
What's tough is being good every day.
—**WILLIE MAYS**

If you can react the same way to winning and losing,
that's a big accomplishment. That quality is important because
it stays with you the rest of your life, and there's going to be a life
after tennis that's a lot longer than your tennis life.
—**CHRIS EVERT**

Don't let what you cannot do interfere with what you can do.
—**JOHN WOODEN**

You are never a loser until you quit trying.
—**MIKE DITKA**

If you don't invest very much, then defeat doesn't hurt very much
and winning is not very exciting.
—**DICK VERMEIL**

•

The spirit, the will to win, and the will to excel
are the things that endure. These qualities are so much
more important than the events that occur.
—**VINCE LOMBARDI**

•

The difference between the impossible and
the possible lies in a man's determination.
—**TOMMY LASORDA**

•

There are only two options regarding commitment; you're either in
or you're out. There's no such thing as life in-between.
—**PAT RILEY**

•

The difference between a successful person and others is not a lack of
strength, not a lack of knowledge, but rather in a lack of will.
—**VINCE LOMBARDI**

The more you sweat in practice, the less you bleed in battle.
—SOURCE UNKNOWN

An athlete cannot run with money in his pockets.
He must run with hope in his heart and dreams in his head.
—EMIL ZATOPEK

The difference between involvement and commitment is like
ham and eggs. The chicken is involved; the pig is committed.
—MARTINA NAVRATILOVA

In play there are two pleasures for your choosing.
One is winning, and the other losing.
—LORD BYRON

Pain is nothing compared to what it feels like to quit.
—SOURCE UNKNOWN

I have nothing in common with lazy people who
blame others for their lack of success. Great things come
from hard work and perseverance. No excuses.
—KOBE BRYANT

•

Don't quit. Suffer now and live the rest of your life as a champion.
—MUHAMMAD ALI

•

Circumstances may cause interruptions and delays,
but never lose sight of your goal. Prepare yourself in every way
you can by increasing your knowledge and adding to your experience,
so that you can make the most of opportunity when it occurs.
—MARIO ANDRETTI

•

Be strong in body, clean in mind, lofty in ideals.
—JAMES NAISMITH

•

Winning is about heart, not just legs. It's got to be in the right place.
—LANCE ARMSTRONG

Confidence is the most important single factor in this game,

and no matter how great your natural talent,

there is only one way to obtain and sustain it: work.

— JACK NICKLAUS

•

You have to expect things of yourself before you can do them.

— MICHAEL JORDAN

•

Leadership is a matter of having people look at you and

gain confidence, seeing how you react.

If you're in control, they're in control.

— TOM LANDRY

•

Champions keep playing until they get it right.

— BILLIE KING

You can't put a limit on anything.

The more you dream, the farther you get.

— MICHAEL PHELPS

Confidence is the most important single factor in this game,

and no matter how great your natural talent,

there is only one way to obtain and sustain it: work.

—JACK NICKLAUS

Celebrate what you've accomplished,

but raise the bar a little higher each time you succeed.

—MIA HAMM

The principle is competing against yourself. It's about self-

improvement, about being better than you were the day before.

—STEVE YOUNG

If you don't do what's best for your body,

you're the one who comes up on the short end.

—JULIUS ERVING

Sports do not build character. They reveal it.

—JOHN WOODEN

I've failed over and over and over again in my life and

that is why I succeed.

—MICHAEL JORDAN

Before you can win a game, you have to not lose it.

—CHUCK NOLL

To be a great champion you must believe you are the best.

If you're not, pretend you are.

—MUHAMMAD ALI

Make sure your worst enemy doesn't live between your own two ears.

—LAIRD HAMILTON

If you don't have confidence, you'll always find a way not to win.

—CARL LEWIS

Experience is a hard teacher because she gives the test first,

the lesson afterward.

—VERNON LAW

•

If you can't accept losing, you can't win.

—VINCE LOMBARDI

•

Never let the fear of striking out get in your way.

—BABE RUTH

•

Concentration is a fine antidote to anxiety.

—JACK NICKLAUS

•

Desire is the key to motivation, but it's determination and

commitment to an unrelenting pursuit of your goal—a commitment to

excellence—that will enable you to attain the success you seek.

—MARIO ANDRETTI

The rewards are going to come, but my happiness is

just loving the sport and having fun performing.

—JACKIE JOYNER KERSEE

●

As you walk down the fairway of life you must smell the roses,

for you only get to play one round.

—BEN HOGAN

●

Do you know what my favorite part of the game is?

The opportunity to play.

—MIKE SINGLETARY

●

God gets you to the plate, but once you're there you're on your own.

—TED WILLIAMS

●

I was told over and over again that I would never be successful, that

I was not going to be competitive, and the technique was simply not

going to work. All I could do was shrug and say, we'll just have to see.

—DICK FOSBURY

A good hockey player plays where the puck is.

A great hockey player plays where the puck is going to be.

—WAYNE GRETZKY

●

You owe it to yourself to be the best you can possibly be—

in baseball and in life.

—PETE ROSE

●

Toughness is in the soul and spirit, not in muscles.

—ALEX KARRAS

●

I always felt that my greatest asset was not my physical ability,

it was my mental ability.

—CAITLYN JENNER

●

I figure practice puts your brains in your muscles.

—SAM SNEAD

If winning isn't everything, why do they keep score?
—**VINCE LOMBARDI**

•

When I step onto the court, I don't have to think about anything.
If I have a problem off the court, I find that after I play,
my mind is clearer and I can come up with a better solution.
It's like therapy. It relaxes me and allows me to solve problems.
—**MICHAEL JORDAN**

•

The ideal attitude is to be physically loose and mentally tight.
—**ARTHUR ASHE**

•

My thoughts before a big race are usually pretty simple. I tell myself:
Get out of the blocks, run your race, stay relaxed. If you run your race,
you'll win . . . channel your energy. Focus.
—**CARL LEWIS**

•

Mental will is a muscle that needs exercise, just like muscles of the body.
—**LYNN JENNINGS**

Luck? Sure. But only after long practice and only with
the ability to think under pressure.
— **BABE DIDRIKSON ZAHARIAS**

•

Wisdom is always an overmatch for strength.
— **PHIL JACKSON**

•

The road to Easy Street goes through the sewer.
— **JOHN MADDEN**

Chapter

· · · · · · · · · · · ·

XVI

On the Arts

Love of beauty is taste. The creation of beauty is art.

—RALPH WALDO EMERSON

•

If you ask me what I came into this life to do, I will tell you:

I came to live out loud.

—EMILE ZOLA

•

Creativity takes courage.

—HENRI MATISSE

•

The true work of art is but a shadow of the divine perfection.

—MICHELANGELO DI LODOVICO BUONARROTI SIMONI

•

Every good painter paints what he is.

—REMBRANDT VAN RIJN

•

The only time I feel alive is when I'm painting.

—ANDY WARHOL

Simonides calls painting silent poetry, and poetry speaking painting.
—**PLUTARCH**

•

Every artist was first an amateur.
—**RALPH WALDO EMERSON**

•

I have always tried to hide my own efforts and wished my works to
have the lightness and joyousness of a springtime which never lets
anyone suspect the labors it cost.
—**HENRI MATISSE**

•

Painting is stronger than me, it makes me do its bidding.
—**PABLO PICASSO**

•

The pain passes, but the beauty remains.
—**PIERRE-AUGUSTE RENOIR**
(WHEN CRIPPLED WITH ARTHRITIS)

An artist is not paid for his labor but for his vision.

—JAMES MCNEILL WHISTLER

Every artist dips his brush in his own soul and

paints his own nature into his pictures.

—HENRY WARD BEECHER

The artist is a receptacle for emotions that come from all over the place:

from the sky, from the earth, from a scrap of paper,

from a passing shape, from a spider's web.

—PABLO PICASSO

The secret of life is in art.

—OSCAR WILDE

Fine art is that in which the hand, the head, and the heart go together.

—JOHN RUSKIN

Art is a human activity having for its purpose the transmission to
others of the highest and best feelings.
—**LEO TOLSTOY**

•

In art, the hand can never execute anything higher
than the heart can inspire.
—**RALPH WALDO EMERSON**

•

I am enough of an artist to draw freely upon my imagination.
Imagination is more important than knowledge. Knowledge is limited.
Imagination encircles the world.
—**ALBERT EINSTEIN**

•

Art enables us to find ourselves and lose ourselves at the same time.
—**THOMAS MERTON**

•

Art is much less important than life, but what a poor life without it.
—**ROBERT MOTHERWELL**

It is through Art and through Art only that we can realize our
perfection; through Art and Art only that we can shield
ourselves from the sordid perils of actual existence.
—OSCAR WILDE

•

I do not literally paint that table, but the emotion it produces upon me.
—HENRI MATISSE

•

Love the art in yourself, not yourself in the art.
—CONSTANTIN STANISLAVSKI

•

I don't say everything, but I paint everything.
—PABLO PICASSO

•

Art is the window to man's soul.
Without it, he would never be able to see beyond his immediate world;
nor could the world see the man within.
—CLAUDIA "LADY BIRD" JOHNSON

In music the passions enjoy themselves.
—FRIEDRICH NIETZSCHE

●

After silence, that which comes nearest to expressing the inexpressible

is music.
—ALDOUS HUXLEY

●

Where words fail, music speaks.
—HANS CHRISTIAN ANDERSEN

●

Without a song, each day would be a century.
—MAHALIA JACKSON

●

There's no such thing as a wrong note as long as you're singing it.
—PETE SEEGER

●

Music expresses that which cannot be put into words and

that which cannot remain silent.
—VICTOR HUGO

Music is a higher revelation than all wisdom and philosophy. Music is
the electrical soil in which the spirit lives, thinks, and invents.
—LUDWIG VAN BEETHOVEN

If you look deep enough you will see music;
the heart of nature being everywhere music.
—THOMAS CARLYLE

A song will outlive all sermons in the memory.
—HENRY GILES

Music is a moral law. It gives soul to the universe,
wings to the mind, flight to the imagination, and
charm and gaiety to life and to everything.
—PLATO

Music hath charms to soothe a savage breast,
to soften rocks or bend a knotted oak.
—WILLIAM CONGREVE

The music that really turns me on is either

running toward God or away from God.

Both recognize the pivot, that God is at the center of the jaunt.

—BONO

•

What we play is life.

—LOUIS ARMSTRONG

•

Without music, life would be a mistake.

—FRIEDRICH NIETZSCHE

•

Great music is that which penetrates the ear with facility

and leaves the memory with difficulty.

Magical music never leaves the memory.

—SIR THOMAS BEECHAM

•

Music is well said to be the speech of angels.

—THOMAS CARLYLE

Music washes away from the soul the dust of everyday life.
—BERTHOLD AUERBACH

Do you know that our soul is composed of harmony?
—LEONARDO DA VINCI

In my paintings, I wish to create a spiritual remedy,
similar to a comfortable armchair
which provides rest from physical expectation for the spiritually
working, the businessman, as well as the artist.
—HENRI MATISSE

Take a music bath once or twice a week for a few seasons, and you will
find that it is to the soul what the water bath is to the body.
—OLIVER WENDELL HOLMES

I think music in itself is healing. It's an explosive expression of humanity.
It's something we are all touched by. No matter what culture we're from,
everyone loves music.
—BILLY JOEL

Music melts all the separate parts of our bodies together.
—**ANAÏS NIN**

Just as Jesus created wine from water, we humans are capable
of transmuting emotion into music.
—**CARLOS SANTANA**

Music can change the world because it can change people.
—**BONO**

Music does bring people together. It allows us to experience the same
emotions. No matter what language we speak, what color we are, the
form of our politics or the expression of our love and our faith, music
proves: We are the same.
—**JOHN DENVER**

Music gives a soul to the universe, wings to the mind,
flight to the imagination, and life to everything.
—**PLATO**

Music is by far the most wonderful method we have to remind us
each day of the power of personal accomplishment.
—CHRIS S. SALAZAR

Music, the greatest good that mortals know,
and all of heaven we have below.
—JOSEPH ADDISON

A bird does not sing because it has an answer.
It sings because it has a song.
—CHINESE PROVERB

I don't want people who want to dance;
I want people who have to dance.
—GEORGE BALANCHINE

I should not believe in a God who does not dance.
—FRIEDRICH NIETZSCHE

We ought to dance with rapture that we might be alive . . .

and part of the living, incarnate cosmos.

—D. H. LAWRENCE

◉

The dance: a minimum of explanation, a minimum of anecdotes,

and a maximum of sensations.

—MAURICE BÉJART

◉

Dance first. Think later. It's the natural order.

—SAMUEL BECKETT

◉

The truest expression of a people is in its dance and in its music.

Bodies never lie.

—AGNES DE MILLE

◉

Dancing can reveal all the mystery that music conceals.

—CHARLES BAUDELAIRE

Dance is like life, it exists as you're flitting through it,

and when it's over, it's done.

—**JEROME ROBBINS**

To watch us dance is to hear our hearts speak.

—**INDIAN PROVERB**

Those who dance are considered insane

by those who can't hear the music.

—**GEORGE CARLIN**

Dance is the hidden language of the soul.

—**MARTHA GRAHAM**

I see dance being used as communication between body and soul,

to express what is too deep to find for words.

—**RUTH ST. DENIS**

Dancing is the loftiest, the most moving, the most beautiful of the arts,

because it is no mere translation or abstraction from life;

it is life itself.

—HAVELOCK ELLIS

Dance for yourself, if someone understands good.

If not then no matter, go right on doing what you love.

—LOIS HURST

Kids: they dance before they learn there is anything that isn't music.

—WILLIAM STAFFORD

Always be a poet, even in prose.

—CHARLES BAUDELAIRE

Poetry is a phantom script telling how rainbows are made

and why they go away.

—CARL SANDBURG

The poet is the priest of the invisible.
—WALLACE STEVENS

⊛

My poems are hymns of praise to the glory of life.
—EDITH SITWELL

⊛

Great poetry is always written by somebody
straining to go beyond what he can do.
—BOB DYLAN

⊛

Poetry is just the evidence of life. If your life is burning well,
poetry is just the ash.
—LEONARD COHEN

⊛

It is in literature that the concrete outlook of humanity
receives its expression.
—ALFRED NORTH WHITEHEAD

Literature adds to reality, it does not simply describe it. It enriches the necessary competencies that daily life requires and provides; and in this respect, it irrigates the deserts that our lives have already become.

—C. S. LEWIS

Literature is a luxury; fiction is a necessity.

—G. K. CHESTERTON

Literature is where I go to explore the highest and lowest places in human society and in the human spirit, where I hope to find not absolute truth but the truth of the tale, of the imagination and of the heart.

—SALMAN RUSHDIE

All good books are alike in that they are truer than if they had really happened and after you are finished reading one you will feel that all that happened to you and afterwards it all belongs to you; the good and the bad, the ecstasy, the remorse, and sorrow, the people and the places and how the weather was.

—ERNEST HEMINGWAY

The crown of literature is poetry.

—W. SOMERSET MAUGHAM

•

My task which I am trying to achieve is, by the power of the written word, to make you hear, to make you feel—it is, before all, to make you see. That—and no more, and it is everything. If I succeed, you shall find there according to your deserts: encouragement, consolation, fear, charm—all you demand; and, perhaps, also that glimpse of truth for which you have forgotten to ask.

—JOSEPH CONRAD

•

The duty of literature is to note what counts, and to light up what is suited to the light. If it ceases to choose and to love, it becomes like a woman who gives herself without preference.

—ANATOLE FRANCE

•

What is wonderful about great literature is that it transforms the man who reads it towards the condition of the man who wrote.

—E. M. FORSTER

Reading maketh a full man, conference a ready man,

and writing an exact man.

—SIR FRANCIS BACON

•

When once the itch of literature comes over a man,

nothing can cure it but the scratching of a pen.

—SAMUEL LOVER

•

While thought exists, words are alive and literature becomes an escape,

not from, but into living.

—CYRIL CONNOLLY

•

It is the writer's privilege to help man endure by lifting his heart.

—WILLIAM FAULKNER

•

No matter how old you get, if you can keep the desire to be creative,

you're keeping the man-child alive.

—JOHN CASSAVETES

Chapter

· · · · · · · · · · · · ·

XVII

On Government and Politics

Writing laws is easy, but governing is difficult.

—LEO TOLSTOY

•

Is life so dear or peace so sweet as to be purchased at the price of chains
and slavery? Forbid it, Almighty God! I know not what course others
may take, but as for me, give me liberty, or give me death!

—PATRICK HENRY

•

And so, my fellow Americans: ask not what your country can
do for you—ask what you can do for your country. . . .
My fellow citizens of the world: ask not what America will do for you,
but what together we can do for the freedom of man.

—JOHN F. KENNEDY

•

The right way is not always the popular and easy way. Standing for
right when it is unpopular is a true test of moral character.

—MARGARET CHASE SMITH

Government is a trust, and the officers of the government
are trustees; and both the trust and the trustees
are created for the benefit of the people.
—**HENRY CLAY**

•

The peril of this nation is not in any foreign foe!
We, the people, are its power, its peril, and its hope!
—**CHARLES EVANS HUGHES**

•

We shall fight on the seas and oceans . . . we shall defend our island,
whatever the cost may be. We shall fight on the beaches, we shall fight
on the landing grounds, we shall fight in the fields and in the streets,
we shall fight in the hills; we shall never surrender.
—**SIR WINSTON CHURCHILL**

It was we, the people; not we, the white male citizens; nor yet we, the male citizens; but we, the whole people, who formed the Union. And we formed it, not to give the blessings of liberty, but to secure them; not to the half of ourselves and the half of our posterity, but to the whole people—women as well as men.

—SUSAN B. ANTHONY

We will not be driven by fear into an age of unreason if we dig deep in our history and remember that we are not descended from fearful men, not from men who feared to write, to speak, to associate, and to defend causes which were for the moment unpopular.

—EDWARD R. MURROW

In politics, if you want anything said, ask a man. If you want anything done, ask a woman.

—MARGARET THATCHER

I have fought against white domination and I have fought against black domination. I have cherished the ideal of a democratic and free society in which all persons live together in harmony and with equal opportunities. It is an ideal which I hope to live for and to achieve. But if needs be, it is an ideal for which I am prepared to die.

—**NELSON MANDELA**

The care of human life and happiness, and not their destruction, is the first and only object of good government.

—**THOMAS JEFFERSON**

The very essence of a free government consists in considering offices as public trusts, bestowed for the good of the country, and not for the benefit of an individual or a party.

—**JOHN C. CALHOUN**

There are only two main theories of government in our world.
One rests on righteousness and the other on force. One appeals
to reason, and the other appeals to the sword. One is exemplified
in the republic, the other is represented by despotism.
—CALVIN COOLIDGE

Politics, when it is an art and a service, not an exploitation,
is about acting for an ideal through realities.
—CHARLES DE GAULLE

Observe good faith and justice toward all nations.
Cultivate peace and harmony with all.
—GEORGE WASHINGTON

You can not possibly have a broader basis for any government than
that which includes all the people, with all their rights in their hands,
and with an equal power to maintain their rights.
—WILLIAM LLOYD GARRISON

I do not mistrust the future; I do not fear what is ahead.

For our problems are large, but our heart is larger.

Our challenges are great, but our will is greater.

And if our flaws are endless, God's love is truly boundless.

—GEORGE H. W. BUSH

No one pretends that democracy is perfect or all-wise. Indeed, it has been said that democracy is the worst form of Government except for all those other forms that have been tried from time to time.

—SIR WINSTON CHURCHILL

Divide and rule, the politician cries; unite and lead,

is watchword of the wise.

—JOHANN WOLFGANG VON GOETHE

Today, we do more than celebrate America; we rededicate ourselves to the very idea of America. An idea born in revolution and renewed through two centuries of challenge. An idea tempered by the knowledge that, but for fate, we—the fortunate and the unfortunate— might have been each other. An idea ennobled by the faith that our nation can summon from its myriad diversity the deepest measure of unity. An idea infused with the conviction that America's long heroic journey must go forever upward.

—**BILL CLINTON**

•

That is the best government which desires to make the people happy, and knows how to make them happy.

—**LORD MACAULAY**

•

Our safety, our liberty, depends upon preserving the Constitution of the United States as our fathers made it inviolate. The people of the United States are the rightful masters of both Congress and the courts, not to overthrow the Constitution, but to overthrow the men who pervert the Constitution.

—**ABRAHAM LINCOLN**

In no nation are the fruits of accomplishment more secure.
In no nation is the government more worthy of respect.
No country is more loved by its people. I have an abiding faith
in their capacity, integrity and high purpose. I have no fears
for the future of our country. It is bright with hope.
—**HERBERT HOOVER**

*

They who can give up essential liberty to obtain a little temporary
safety deserve neither liberty nor safety.
—**BENJAMIN FRANKLIN**

*

America was not built on fear. America was built on courage, on
imagination and an unbeatable determination to do the job at hand.
—**HARRY S. TRUMAN**

*

We may have all come on different ships,
but we're in the same boat now.
—**MARTIN LUTHER KING JR.**

The problems of the world cannot possibly be solved by skeptics or cynics whose horizons are limited by the obvious realities. We need men who can dream of things that never were.
— JOHN F. KENNEDY

●

Wars may be fought with weapons, but they are won by men. It is the spirit of men who follow and of the man who leads that gains the victory.
— GEORGE S. PATTON JR.

●

The mystic chords of memory, stretching from every battlefield and patriot grave to every living heart and hearthstone all over this broad land, will yet swell the chorus of the Union, when again touched, as surely they will be, by the better angels of our nature.
— ABRAHAM LINCOLN

●

We must not confuse dissent with disloyalty. When the loyal opposition dies, I think the soul of America dies with it.
— EDWARD R. MURROW

My oath is not so different from the pledge we all make to the flag that waves above and that fills our hearts with pride. They are the words of citizens and they represent our greatest hope. You and I, as citizens, have the power to set this country's course. You and I, as citizens, have the obligation to shape the debates of our time—not only with the votes we cast, but with the voices we lift in defense of our most ancient values and enduring ideals.

—BARACK OBAMA

True patriotism hates injustice in its own land more than anywhere else.

—CLARENCE DARROW

I know no safe depository of the ultimate powers of the society but the people themselves; and if we think them not enlightened enough to exercise their control with a wholesome discretion, the remedy is not to take it from them, but to inform their discretion by education. This is the true corrective of abuses of constitutional power.

—THOMAS JEFFERSON

I apprehend no danger to our country from a foreign foe.

Our destruction, should it come at all, will be from another quarter.

From the inattention of the people to the concerns of their

government, from their carelessness and negligence,

I must confess that I do apprehend some danger.

—DANIEL WEBSTER

•

There is no good reason why we should fear the future,

but there is every reason why we should face it seriously,

neither hiding from ourselves the gravity of the problems

before us nor fearing to approach these problems with the unbending,

unflinching purpose to solve them aright.

—THEODORE ROOSEVELT

•

An imbalance between rich and poor is the oldest and

most fatal ailment of all republics.

—PLUTARCH

•

Obedience to lawful authority is the foundation of manly character.

—ROBERT E. LEE

The first method for estimating the intelligence of a ruler

is to look at the men he has around him.

—NICCOLÒ MACHIAVELLI

When the Declaration of Independence was first read in public and

the Liberty Bell was sounded in celebration, a witness said, "It rang as

if it meant something." In our time it means something still.

—GEORGE W. BUSH

Only an alert and knowledgeable citizenry can compel the

proper meshing of the huge industrial and military machinery

of defense with our peaceful methods and goals,

so that security and liberty may prosper together.

—DWIGHT D. EISENHOWER

Democracy is worth dying for, because it's the most deeply honorable

form of government ever devised by man.

—RONALD REAGAN

The proper function of a government is to make it easy for the people
to do good, and difficult for them to do evil.
—DANIEL WEBSTER

Democracy cannot succeed unless those who express
their choice are prepared to choose wisely. The real safeguard
of democracy, therefore, is education.
—FRANKLIN D. ROOSEVELT

Being democratic is not enough, a majority cannot turn what is wrong
into right. In order to be considered truly free, countries must also have
a deep love of liberty and an abiding respect for the rule of law.
—MARGARET THATCHER

I have a dream that one day this nation will rise up and live out the true meaning of its creed: "We hold these truths to be self-evident, that all men are created equal". . . .

And when this happens, and when we allow freedom ring, when we let it ring from every village and every hamlet, from every state and every city, we will be able to speed up that day when all of God's children, black men and white men, Jews and Gentiles, Protestants and Catholics, will be able to join hands and sing in the words of the old Negro spiritual: "Free at last! Free at last! Thank God Almighty, we are free at last!"

—**MARTIN LUTHER KING JR.**

SELECTED QUOTED SOURCES

* * * * * * * * * * * * * *

Aaron, Hank (b. 1934), American professional baseball player

Abdul-Jabbar, Kareem (b. 1947), American professional basketball player

Adams, Abigail (1744–1818), American writer and wife of John Adams

Adams, John (1735–1826), second US president

Adams, John Quincy (1767–1848), sixth US president, son of John Adams

Addison, Joseph (1672–1719), Englishessayist, poet, statesman

Ade, George (1866–1944), American playwright and newspaper columnist

Aeschylus (525–456 B.C.), Greek tragic dramatist

Aesop (c. 500 B.C.–?), Greek fabulist

Alcott, Bronson (1799–1888), American educational and social reformer

Alcott, Louisa May (1832–1888), American novelist

Ali, Muhammad (1942–2016), American prizefighter

Alighieri, Dante (1265–1321), Italian poet

Allen, George (1918–1990), American professional football coach

Amiel, Henri-Frédéric (1821–1881), Swiss philosopher and poet

Andretti, Mario (b. 1940), Italian-American auto racing driver

Angelou, Maya (b. 1928), American author, poet, and composer

Annan, Kofi (b. 1938), Ghanaian diplomat and United Nations secretary-general

Anthony, Susan B. (1820–1906), American women's suffrage leader

Aristophanes (c. 448 B.C.–c. 388 B.C.), Athenian playwright

Aristotle (384 B.C.–322 B.C.), Greek philosopher

Armstrong, Louis (1901–1971), American jazz musician

Ashe, Arthur (1943–1993), American tennis player

Assisi, Saint Francis of (1182–1226), founder of the Franciscan order

Astor, Lady Nancy (1879–1964), English politician

Aurelius, Marcus (121 A.D.–180 A.D.), Roman emperor

Austen, Jane (1775–1817), British writer

Bach, Richard (b. 1936), American writer

Bacon, Sir Francis (1561–1626), statesman, philosopher, and essayist

Balanchine, George (1904–1983), American ballet choreographer

Baldwin, James (1924–1987), American critic and writer

Balzac, Honoré de (1799–1850), French writer

Bannister, Sir Roger (b. 1929), British long-distance runner
Barrie, Sir James Matthew (1860–1937), British writer
Barton, Bruce (1886–1967), American congressman
Baruch, Bernard M. (1870–1965), American political advisor and financial investor
Beecher, Henry Ward (1813–1887), American clergyman and social reformer
Beethoven, Ludwig von (1770–1827), German composer
Berlin, Irving (1888–1989), American popular music composer
Bidpai (?) supposed name of the author of the Sanskrit Panchatantra fables
Bierce, Ambrose (1842–1914), American journalist
Billings, Josh (1818–1885), American humorous essayist
Bird, Larry (b. 1956), American professional basketball player
Birkenhead, F. E. Smith, Lord (1872–1930), British politician
Blake, William (1757–1827), British poet
Bloom, Amy (b. 1953), American psychotherapist and writer
Bonaparte, Napoléon (1769–1821), French general and emperor
Bono (b. 1960), pseudonym of Paul David Hewson, Irish musician and philanthropist
Bradbury, Ray (1920–2012), American science-fiction writer
Bradstreet, Anne (1612–1672), colonial American poet
Brothers, Dr. Joyce (b. 1929), American psychologist
Brown, H. Jackson, Jr. (b. 1940), American author
Browning, Elizabeth Barrett (1806–1861), British poet
Browning, Robert (1812–1889), British poet
Bryan, William Jennings (1860–1925), American lawyer and politician
Bryant, Kobe (b. 1978), American basketball player
Bryant, William Cullen (1794–1878), American poet and newspaper editor
Buck, Pearl (1892–1973), American missionary and writer
Buddha, Siddhártha Gautama (c. 563 B.C.–c. 483 B.C.), founder of Buddhism
Buffett, Warren (b. 1930), American businessman, investor, and philanthropist
Burke, Edmund (1729–1797), British political writer and statesman
Burns, George (1896–1996), American vaudeville, radio, and television performer
Burns, Robert (1759–1796), Scottish poet
Buscaglia, Leo (1924–1998), American educator
Bush, George H. W. (b. 1924), forty-first US president
Bush, George W. (b. 1946), forty-third US president, son of George H. W. Bush
Butterworth, Eric (1916–2003), American clergyman and author
Byron, George Gordon, Lord (1788–1824), English romantic poet

Campbell, Joseph (1904–1987), American mythologist

Camus, Albert (1913–1960), French existential philosopher and writer

Cantor, Eddie (1892–1964), American entertainer

Carlyle, Thomas (1795–1881), British historian

Carnegie, Dale (1888–1955), American self-improvement author

Carroll, Lewis, pseudonym of Charles Lutwidge Dodson (1832–1898), British writer

Carver, George Washington (1864–1943), American agriculturalist and inventor

Cassavetes, John (1929–1989), Greek-American film director, actor and screenwriter

Castaneda, Carlos (1925–1998), American anthropologist and author

Cervantes, Miguel de (1547–1616), Spanish writer

Chamberlain, Wilt (1936–1999), American professional basketball player

Chávez, César (1927–1993), American agrarian labor leader

Chesterton, G. K. (1974–1936), English author

Child, Julia (1912–2004), American chef, author, and television personality

Christie, Agatha (1890–1976), English mystery writer

Churchill, Sir Winston (1874–1965), English prime minister

Cicero, Marcus Tullius (106 B.C.–43 B.C.), Roman orator

Clark, Tom (1899–1977), US Supreme Court jurist

Clinton, Hillary Rodham (b. 1947), US political figure

Coleridge, Samuel Taylor (1772–1834), English romantic poet

Colette, Sidonie-Gabrielle (1873–1954), French novelist

Confucius (c. 551 B.C.–479 B.C.), Chinese philosopher

Connolly, Cyril (1903–1974), British literary critic and writer

Conrad, Joseph (1857–1924), British novelist

Cooke, Alistair (1908–2004), British-American journalist and radio/TV personality

Coolidge, Calvin (1872–1933), thirtieth U.S. president

Crews, Harry (1935–2012), American novelist and short story writer

Crisp, Quentin (1908–1999), English autobiographer

Crumb, Robert (b. 1943), social and political cartoonist

cummings, e. e. (1894–1962), American poet

Da Vinci, Leonardo (1492–1519), Italian artist and innovator

Dalí, Salvador (1904–1989), Spanish surrealist artist

Darrow, Clarence (1857–1938), American lawyer

Davis, Bette (1908–1989), American film actress

de Bussy-Rabutin, Comte Roger (1618–1693), French satirical writer

De Vries, Peter (1910–1993), American author and humorist

Denver, John (1943–1997), American singer and songwriter
Descartes, René (1596–1650), French philosopher and mathematician
Dickens, Charles (1812–1870), English novelist
Dickinson, Emily (1830–1886), American poet
Disraeli, Benjamin (1804–1881), British prime minister and author
Ditka, Mike (b. 1939), American professional football player and coach
Donne, John (1572–1631), British metaphysical poet
Douglass, Frederick (1817–1895), American abolitionist, author, and orator
Dowd, Maureen (b. 1952), American columnist and author
Dryden, John (1631–1700), English poet laureate
Duncan, Tim (b. 1976), American professional basketball player
Dylan, Bob (b. 1941), American singer and songwriter
Edison, Thomas Alva (1847–1931), American inventor
Einstein, Albert (1879–1955), Austrian-American theoretical physicist
Eisenhower, Dwight David (1890–1969), thirty-fourth US president
Eliot, George, pseudonym of Mary Ann Evans (1819–1880), English novelist
Eliot, T. S. (1885–1968), British poet
Ellington, Duke (1899–1974), American jazz musician
Ellis, Havelock (1859–1939), English physician, author, and social reformer
Emerson, Ralph Waldo (1803–1882), American philosopher and poet
Epictetus (c. 50 A.D. –c. 138 A.D.), Phrygian stoic philosopher
Euripides (c. 480 B.C.–406 B.C.), Greek dramatist
Evert, Chris (b. 1954), American tennis player
Faulkner, William (1897–1962), American author
Fitzgerald, F. Scott (1896–1940), American novelist
Forbes, Malcolm (1919–1990), American magazine publisher
Ford, Henry (1863–1947), American automobile manufacturer
Forster, E(dward) M(organ) (1879–1970), British author
Franklin, Benjamin (1706–1790), American statesman and writer
Freud, Sigmund (1856–1939), neurologist, founder of psychoanalysis
Frost, Robert (1874–1963), American poet
Fuller, Thomas (1608–1661), English clergyman and author
Galbraith, John Kenneth (b. 1908), American economist and public official
Galilei, Galileo (1564–1642), Italian astronomer and physicist
Gandhi, Mohandas (1869–1948), Indian nonviolent nationalist
Geisel, Theodore, see Seuss, Dr.

Getty, J. Paul (1892–1976), American industrialist

Gibbon, Edward (1737–1794), British historian

Gibran, Kahlil (1883–1931), Lebanese-American poet and novelist

Gide, André (1869–1951), French writer

Goethe, Johann Wolfgang von (1749–1832), German poet, dramatist, and novelist

Goldsmith, Oliver (c. 1730–1774), British-Irish author and dramatist

Graham, Billy (b. 1918), American evangelical clergyman

Greene, Graham (1904–1991), English novelist and playwright

Gretzky, Wayne (b. 1961), Canadian ice-hockey player

Guthrie, Woody (1912–1967), American folk singer and composer

Hagen, Walter (1892–1969), American golfer

Halas, George (1895–1983), American professional football coach and team owner

Hamilton, Alexander (1755 or 1757–1804), American statesman

Hamilton, Laird (b. 1964), American surfer

Hamm, Mia (b. 1972), American soccer player

Hammarskjöld, Dag (1905–1961), Secretary-General of the United Nations

Hand, Learned (1872–1961), American jurist

Hardy, Thomas (1840–1928), English novelist

Hawking, Stephen (b. 1942), British theoretical physicist

Hawthorne, Nathaniel (1804–1864), American writer

Hayes, Helen (1900–1993), American stage and film actress

Hazlitt, William (1778–1830), British essayist

Heatter, Gabriel (1890–1972), American radio commentator

Helú, Carlos Slim (b. 1940), Mexican businessman and philanthropist

Hemingway, Ernest (1899–1961), American writer

Henry, Patrick (1736–1799), American statesman

Hesse, Herman (1877–1962), German novelist and poet

Hill, Napoleon (1883–1970), American impresario and author

Hillel the Elder [often called Rabbi Hillel] (c. 110 B.C.–10 A.D.), Babylonian Jewish scholar

Hinton, S. E. (b. 1948), American novelist

Hoffer, Eric (1902–1983), American longshoreman and author

Holmes, Oliver Wendell Jr. (1841–1935), US Supreme Court justice

Holtz, Lou (b. 1937), American college football coach

Homer (850 B.C.—800 B.C.), Greek poet

Horace (65 B.C.–8 B.C.), Roman poet

Hoyle, Edmond (1672–1769), British card game authority

Huff, Sam (b. 1934), American professional football player
Hughes, Charles Evans (1862–1948), US Supreme Court justice
Hugo, Victor (1802–1825), French writer, poet, and dramatist
Humphrey, Hubert H. (1911–1978), US vice president
Hutchins, Robert (1899–1977), American educator
Huxley, Aldous (1894–1963), British novelist
Inge, William Ralph (1860–1954), British cleric known as Dean Inge
James, William (1842–1910), American psychologist and philosopher
Jefferson, Thomas (1743–1826), third US president
Jerome, Jerome K. (1859 –1927), English writer and humorist
John Paul II, Pope (b. 1920), religious leader
John XXIII, Pope (1881–1963), religious leader
Johnson, Claudia "Lady Bird" (1912–2007), American presidential first lady
Johnson, Samuel (1709–1784), English author
Jones, Mary Harris "Mother" Jones (1837–1930), American labor and community organizer
Jordan, Michael (b. 1963), American basketball player
Joubert, Joseph (1754–1824), French moralist
Jung, Carl (1875–1961), Swiss psychiatrist
Justinian I (c. 482–565), Byzantine emperor and author of the Justinian Code
Kafka, Franz (1883–1924), Bohemian novelist
Kaiser, Henry J. (1882–1967), American industrialist
Kaufman, Bel (1911–2014), American schoolteacher and writer
Keller, Helen (1880–1968), American writer and lecturer
Kennedy, John F. (1917–1963), thirty-fifth US president
Kenny, Elizabeth (1886–1952), Australian nurse and author
Khayyam, Omar (1048–1131), Persian poet and mathematician
Kierkegaard, Søren (1813–1855), Danish philosopher
King, Billie Jean (b. 1943), American tennis player
Kleiser, Grenville (1868–1935), Canadian-American author
Koyczan, Shane (b. 1976), Canadian poet
Kronenberger, Louis (1904–1980), American novelist and critic
Kushner, Rabbi Harold (b. 1935) American rabbi and author
Kyosaki, Robert (b. 1947), American businessman and motivational speaker
Laërtius, Diogenes, third-century Greek biographer
Landers, Ann, pseudonym of Esther Lederer (1918–2002), American advice columnist
Lao Tzu, sixth-century Chinese philosopher

La Rochefoucauld, François de (1613–1680), French essayist and epigram writer
LaPorte, Danielle (b. 1969), Canadian author and entrepreneur
Larsson, Stieg (1954–2004), Swedish mystery novelist
Lawrence, D. H. (1885–1930), British novelist
Lec, Stanislaw (1909–1966), Polish poet
Levinson, Sam (1911–1980), American humorist and television personality
Lewis, C. S. (1898–1963), British writer
Lincoln, Abraham (1809–1865), sixteenth US president
Linkletter, Art (1912–2010), Canadian-American radio and TV personality
Lombardi, Vince (1913–1970), American football coach
Longfellow, Henry Wadsworth (1807–1882), American poet
Loren, Sophia (b. 1934), Italian film actress
Luther, Martin (1483–1546), German leader of the Protestant Reformation
MacArthur, Douglas (1880–1964), American general
Machiavelli, Niccolò (1469–1527), Italian Renaissance author and statesman
Malcolm X (1925–1965), American Muslim minister and social activist
Mandela, Nelson (1918–2013), South African resistance leader and statesman
Mandino, Augustine "Og" (1923–1996), American businessman and author
Mantle, Mickey (1931–1995), American baseball player
Marley, Bob (1945–1981), Jamaican reggae singer
Matisse, Henri (1869–1954), French painter and sculptor
Maugham, W. Somerset (1874–1956), English novelist
Maurois, André (1885–1967), French writer and biographer
Maxwell, John C. (b. 1947), American clergyman, author, and motivational speaker
May, Rollo (1909–1994), American psychologist
Maybie, Hamilton Wright (1846–1916), American essayist and writer
Mays, Willie (b. 1931), American professional baseball player
May-Treanor, Misty (b. 1977), American beach volleyball player
McCartney, Paul (b. 1942), British singer/songwriter, member of The Beatles
McGinley, Phyllis (1905–1978), American poet
McInerney, Jay (b. 1955), American novelist
Melville, Herman (1819–1891), American author
Mencken, H(enry) L(ouis) (1880–1956), American editor and critic
Merton, Thomas (1915–1968), American religious writer
Michelangelo di Lodovico Buonarroti Simoni (1475–1564), Italian artist
Midler, Bette (b. 1944), American singer and actress

Miller, Henry (1891–1980), American writer
Miller, Johnny (b. 1947), American golfer and broadcaster
Milne, A. A. (1882–1956), English author
Milton, John (1608–1674), English poet
Mirabeau, Honoré Gabriel Riqueti, Conte de (1749–1791), French statesman
Molière, pseudonym of Jean-Baptiste Poquelin (1622–1673), French playwright
Monroe, Marilyn (1926–1962), American film actress
Montaigne, Michel de (1533–1592), French essayist
More, Sir Thomas (1478–1535), English lawyer, author, statesman and Catholic saint
Murrow, Edward R. (1908–1965), American journalist and radio broadcaster
Namath, Joe (b. 1943), American professional football player and actor
Navratilova, Martina (b. 1956), Czech-American tennis player
Naylor, Gloria (b. 1950), American writer
Nehru, Jawaharlal (1889–1964), first Indian prime minister
Nicklaus, Jack (b. 1940), American professional golfer
Niebuhr, Reinhold (1892–1971), American theologian
Nietzsche, Friedrich Wilhelm (1844–1900), German philosopher
Nin, Anaïs (1903–1977), French-American writer
Noll, Chuck (1932–2014), American professional football player and coach
Obama, Barack (b. 1961), forty-fourth US president
Ovid (43 B.C.–17 A.D.), Roman poet
Paige, Satchel (1906–1982), American baseball player
Paine, Thomas (1737–1809), Anglo-American political theorist
Palmer, Arnold (b. 1929), American professional golfer
Parkinson, Cyril Northcote (1909–1993), British historian
Pascal, Blaise (1623–1662), French philosopher
Patton, George Smith, Jr. (1885–1945), American military leader
Peale, Norman Vincent (1898–1993), American clergyman
Penick, Harvey (1904–1995), American golf professional and coach
Penny, James Cash (J. C.), (1875–1971), American businessman
Pericles (495 B.C.–429 B.C.), Athenian statesman
Perot, H. Ross (b. 1930), American business executive and presidential candidate
Peter, Laurence J. (1919–1988), American educator and writer
Picasso, Pablo (1881–1973), Spanish artist
Pickens, T. Boone (b. 1928), American businessman and financier
Plato (c. 427 B.C.–347 B.C.), Greek philosopher

Plutarch (c. 46 A.D.–c. 120 A.D.), Greek philosopher and biographer
Proust, Marcel (1871–1922), French writer
Rand, Ayn (1905–1982), Russian-American novelist
Reagan, Ronald (1911–2004), Fortieth U.S. president
Repplier, Agnes (1855–1950), American essayist
Rice, Homer (b. 1927), American college football coach and administrator
Richter, Jean Paul Friedrich (1763–1825), German writer
Rickey, Branch (1881–1965), American baseball executive
Rilke, Rainer Maria (1875–1926), German poet
Robinson, Jackie (1919–1972), American baseball player
Rockefeller, John D., Jr. (1839–1937), American oil magnate and philanthropist
Rogers, Will (1879–1935), American humorist
Rohn, Jim (1930–2009), American motivational speaker
Roosevelt, Eleanor (1884–1962), American presidential first lady and diplomat
Roosevelt, Franklin Delano (1882–1945), thirty-second US president
Roosevelt, Theodore (1858–1919), twenty-sixth US president
Rose, Pete (b. 1941), American baseball player and manager
Rousseau, Jean-Jacques (1712–1778), French philosopher
Rowling, J. K. (1965), British author of the Harry Potter series
Runyon, Damon (1884–1946), American short-story writer and humorist
Rushdie, Salman (b. 1947), British Indian author
Ruskin, John (1819–1900), British art critic
Russell, Bertrand (1872–1970), British philosopher and mathematician
Sabatini, Raphael (1875–1950), Italian-English novelist
Sachs, Rabbi Jonathan, Lord (b. 1947), British rabbi and author
Saint-Exupéry, Antoine de (1900–1944), French writer
Salk, Jonas (1914–1995), American physician and microbiologist
Sandburg, Carl (1878–1967), American writer and poet
Sartre, Jean-Paul (1905–1980), French philosopher
Sawyer, Diane (b. 1945), American television journalist
Schuller, Robert H. (1926–2015), American Protestant clergyman
Schwartz, Morrie (1916–1995), American sociology professor and author
Schweitzer, Albert (1875–1965), Swiss theologian and missionary
Scott, Sir Walter (1771–1832), Scottish poet
Seale, Bobby (b. 1936), American political activist
Seeger, Pete (1919–2024), American poet and folksinger

Seneca, Lucius Annaeus (the Younger), (c. 4 B.C.–65 A.D.), Roman Stoic philosopher

Seuss, Dr. (Theodore Geisel) (1904–1991), American children's book author

Shakespeare, William (1564–1616), English dramatist

Shaw, George Bernard (1856–1950), Irish dramatist and critic

Shelley, Percy Bysshe (1792–1822), British romantic poet

Shula, Don (b. 1930), American professional football player and coach

Silverstein, Shel (1930–1999), American composer, poet, and writer

Sivananda, Swami (1887–1963), Indian physician and sage

Smiles, Samuel (1812–1904), Scottish author and social reformer

Smiley, Tavis (b. 1964), American author and television personality

Smith, Logan Pearsall (1865–1946), British-American essayist and critic

Smith, Margaret Chase (1897–1995), U.S. senator

Snead, Sam (1912–2002), American professional golfer

Socrates (469 B.C.–399 B.C.), Greek philosopher

Sophocles (c. 496 B.C.–406 B.C.), Greek dramatist

Spock, Benjamin (1903–1998), American pediatrician and educator

Stanislavsky, Konstantin (1863–1938), Russian actor and theater director

Steinbeck, John (1902–1968), American novelist

Steinem, Gloria (b. 1934), American feminist writer and editor

Stengel, Charles "Casey" (1890–1975), American baseball manager

Stevenson, Adlai E. (1900–1965), American statesman

Stevenson, Robert Louis (1850–1894), British novelist

Swift, Jonathan (1667–1745), English author and essayist

Syrus, Publilius (b. 42 A.D.), Roman writer

Szasz, Thomas (1920–2012), American psychiatrist and author

Tagore, Rabindranath (1861–1941), Indian poet and author

Talese, Gay (b. 1932), American author and journalist

Teilhard de Chardin, Pierre (1881–1955), French philosopher and theologian

Tennyson, Alfred Lord (1809–1892), English poet

Terence (c. 185 B.C.–159 B.C.), Roman writer of comedies

Teresa, Mother (1910–1997), Albanian-Indian missionary

Thatcher, Margaret (1925–2013), British prime minister

Thoreau, Henry David (1817–1862), American author and naturalist

Thurber, James (1894–1961), American writer and cartoonist

Tolstoy, Leo (1828–1910), Russian novelist and philosopher

Toynbee, Arnold (1889–1975), British historian and philosopher

Trollope, Anthony (1815–1882), English novelist
Truman, Harry S. (1884–1972), thirty-third US president
Trump, Donald J. (b. 1946), American businessman, TV personality, and politician
Twain, Mark, pseudonym of Samuel L. Clemens (1835–1910), American author
Van Gogh, Vincent (1853–1890), Dutch post-impressionist painter
Veblen, Thorstein (1857–1929), American economist and sociologist
Viorst, Judith (b. 1931), American author and journalist
Virgil (Publius Vergilius Maro) (70 B.C.–19 B.C.), Roman poet
Voltaire, pseudonym of François Marie Arouet (1694–1778), French philosopher
Vonnegut, Kurt (1922–2007), American author
Walker, Alice (b. 1944), American novelist
Walpole, Hugh (1884–1941), English author
Walton, Sam (1918–1992), American businessman, founder of Walmart
Warhol, Andy (1928–1987), American pop artist
Warren, Earl (1891–1974), American jurist and politician
Warren, Rick (b. 1954), American clergyman and writer
Washington, Booker T. (1865–1915), American educator and writer
Washington, George (1732–1799), first US president
Watson, Thomas, Sr. (1874–1956), American business leader, IBM chairman
Webster, Daniel (1782–1852), American orator and statesman
White, E. B. (1899–1985), American writer
Whitehead, Alfred North (1861–1947), British mathematician and philosopher
Whitman, Walt (1819–1892), American poet
Whittier, John Greenleaf (1807–1892), American poet
Wiesel, Elie (1928–2016), Romanian-American writer and Holocaust survivor
Wilkinson, Charles "Bud" (1916–1994), American college football coach and politician
Wilcox, Ella Wheeler (1860–1919), American poet and author
Wilde, Oscar (1854–1900), Irish dramatist
Wilder, Thornton (1897–1975), American novelist and dramatist
Wilson, Woodrow (1856–1924), twenty-eighth US president
Winfrey, Oprah (b. 1954), American talk-show host and producer
Wooden, John R. (1910–2010), American college basketball coach
Woodward, Joanne (b. 1930), American film actress
Woolf, Virginia (1882–1941), English novelist and essayist
Wordsworth, William (1770–1850), British romantic poet
Wright, Frank Lloyd (1869–1959), American architect

Yeats, William Butler (1865–1939), Irish poet
Zaharias, Babe Didrikson (1911–1956), golf and track and field athlete
Zatopek, Emil (1922–2000), Czechoslovakian long-distance runner
Ziglar, Hilary "Zig" (1926–2012), American author and motivational speaker
Zola, Emile (1840–1902), French novelist and essayist